Refusing to Grow II

The mother that took out $1,000,000 in loans, because she couldn't fire her son.

A. Ruben

Printed in the United States of America.

Refusing to Grow 2: the mother took out $1,000,000 in loans, because she couldn't fire him / A. Ruben

ISBN: 978-0-9754590-3-4

Ickynicks Publishing

Front Cover by Adam Zillins

The following story is based upon actual events and people. However the timeline of events has been compressed and edited to accommodate the story and its characters. Any similarity of dramatized characters, incidents, companies, or attributes to any actual person, living or dead, or to any actual event or to any existing organization is entirely coincidental and unintentional.

Cast of Characters:

Victor – President as well as husband to Barbara, he will ignore his son's arrogance until it is too late.

Barbara "Barb" – Head of Finance, she will argue with her son daily and will eventually take out over a million dollars in loans in order to save her retirement.

Tony – The son of Victor and Barb, he believes teamwork is defined as everyone listening to him. Often re-framing reality to his liking, he will demand the final say in all decisions as well as use a charity movement to advance his agenda for company succession.

Arthur – Hired as a sales agent, he will earn the respect of his co-workers as well as the affection of Sallie, the daughter of Victor and Barb. He will however conflict with Tony's ambitions and vision for the company.

Sallie – Sister to Tony, she will make the first move towards Arthur as well as the last, ending their relationship by putting her happiness second to her brother's.

Antonio – Brother to Victor, he will become very disturbed by his nephew's obsession to succeed his parents.

Frank – The superintendent, he will be suspended by Tony for disagreeing and eventually retire once the "writing is on the wall."

Troy – A childhood friend of Tony, he will be hired to replace Frank. However, he will align with Arthur and Frank and will quit once the former is dismissed.

Joe – A technician hired by Tony, who will become the subject of heated debate owing to clause that gives him ten additional hours of guaranteed overtime per week.

Amanda – Responsible for Accounts Receivable, she will ultimately be fired by Tony for insubordination for her inability to read his mind.

Tom – The last in a long line of business coaches hired by Tony, he will instead align with Barb and Arthur and leverage his Fortune 500 contacts to assert his expertise over Tony's lofty ideas.

The $5 Million Contract – At an incredible profit of $1,400,000 this deal by Arthur will be the largest the company has ever earned, but unfortunately Tony will reject it for a multitude of bitter reasons including that it wasn't his.

Acknowledgements

The author wishes to thank the following for their support, Lynn, Marilyn, Alex, Sara, Mike and Rochelle. Thank you very much for your assistance in making this work possible.

The following is based on a true story.

Chapters

E. The Legal Fight

His industrialism will be rewarded by the respect of his team, the owners, and even his competition in the market; as he models high standards, transparency and opens lines of communication he will be faced with increasingly more toil from the owner's son, who attempts to undermine him at every turn; with a magnetic personality, this individual will endeavor to not just take over the company but also capitalize on the sufferings of others after a national disaster.

Throughout this tug-of-war for leadership, Arthur will strive to unleash the power within his team while the other will endeavor to only better himself; from an office to a company car, he will bit by bit make every department report to him instead of Arthur. But whereas Arthur praised the efforts of others the owner's son will only cheer himself on.

Refusing to Grow II will once again show the failures of leadership and the stumbles needed to grow.

Preface

Arthur had hoped to be a teacher, but as the recession worsened his chances diminished. Rejected for want of experience and against nearly three thousand other applicants for one teaching job he took a sales job.

This sequel to *Refusing to Grow* is more a prequel, chronicling Arthur's experience before Cleveland. Here he was in Los Angeles beginning his quasi-adventure in sales and just so happening to make quite the impression on his bosses, a couple, as well as their daughter. With more responsibilities, Arthur proved an adept manager and eventually joined the executive team. As his leadership in the company blossomed so did his relationship with the daughter; it was not to last. His success collided with the owner's other child, their son, whose pompous attitude and inflated sense of self-importance threatened to shatter everything; in the course of two years, the future of the company will be decided.

Under Arthur's leadership, the company will grow from $2.6 million to an astonishing $9.6 million; the experiences in LA will forever change Arthur as he learns how to be an effective administrator, cope with drama, and transform a stagnant company into a leader of its market.

Note to the Reader

The following chronological series of semi-disconnected incidents are based on true events and characters, which capture certain personalities perhaps too ridiculous to imagine. Yet, they are neither exaggerations nor embellishments.

A. Ruben

In his latest display of brilliant stupidly he had hired a technician named Joe, and unilaterally decided it was a wise decision to include two clauses into the contract that were anything but financially sound. The first clause stipulated that Joe was promised forty hours guaranteed, regardless of whether there was work to be done or not. Hence, even if he only worked thirty hours a week he was still contractually entitled to be paid for forty. In fact, Joe could have- technically speaking- come to work, punched in, and then left for the day. Barb's only saving grace was that Joe believed in earning an honest living, and so she had something to bill for his time.

The other clause guaranteed Joe ten hours a week of overtime. Again, whether he worked or not he was paid this. Thus, Joe was actually being paid 50 hours a week, much to Barb's exasperation. While she presumably could fight the legality of it, since neither her husband nor her had actually signed the contract, Tony insisted he was an officer of the company, and therefore fully authorized to endorse any binding contract.

Barb was livid. She slammed her hard fist on the desk. "What the hell is wrong with him," she said aloud rhetorically. "How dumb could he possibly be?"

Chapter 1

The Heir Apparent

Barb resigned to the sad facts.

"My son will be the death of this company," she said early one morning. It was 8:02 AM and she was already ready to go home; Arthur was seated across from her. It was their daily morning meeting, and lately she was getting more frustrated. It seemed like his antics were getting worse.

For the last four years, her son, Tony, had been employed at the company and while he had been learning his humility was wanting. Nearly every decision of his had cost the company money, and yet he failed to accept any responsibility. Instead, he simply pointed the finger; he neither recognized his mistakes nor felt he was anything less than a genius, believing firmly in his destiny as CEO.

Company Culture

She had no patience left. She didn't care if others heard her. Se had had it with him, and his absurdities. She cursed ever giving birth to him. And this was perhaps why she trusted Arthur, who was in fact dating her daughter:

Over the last few months the two had grown quite close and Barb was quick to embrace him as her future son-in-law. He was a good worker, smart, and able to take directions; he delegated well, and bit-by-bit was advising her on just about everything in the company; he was her senior advisor. She brought him in on operational as well as financial matters, giving him more authority than perhaps Tony liked; it seemed the more responsibility Arthur got the more unsettled Tony became. But Arthur was tactful, always trying to find the middle ground, compromising as often as helping resolve conflict.

She turned to him. "If I had wanted one of his business coaches in here I would have asked them, but instead I asked for you." She trusted Arthur, giving him access to projection sheets, fiscal reports, and anything to help him achieve her dream of ending the stagnation; for 15 years the company had hovered at about $3 million, never being able to grow above it. Once it did, but only narrowly.

"I want us to grow, and I want you do it for us."

"That's the plan." His smile was genuine.

But it seemed the only obstacle in that path was Tony. The last four years he had done nothing but hurt the company, even though he denied the accusations. "All I need him to do is make me money," she said, loathing his very existence. And it was partially true. Tony was very big in self-promotion. He had made himself the sales manager, given himself an office, a company car, a company credit card, and then decided one day it was just easier to ride the blood wagon; he slept in late, did as little work as possible, and happily collected his paycheck. Barb couldn't recall just how many times she dragged him out of bed.

Lazy and useless, she compared him to a broken styptic system; a bursting cesspool was more preferable than him or his ideas that did nothing but cost money and waste time. And yet, if Tony didn't get his way he went into a tantrum like a child. To make matters worse, he exercised powers he didn't have: he fired employees without notice, expunging the company of its talent and manpower; he axed the general manager and the company's inside accountant, both upstanding employees and both without any consultation from his parents; he simply decided one day that they had to go, falsely accusing them of conspiring to embezzle.

When it had had happened it came as much of a shock to the two of them as it had for Barb, who was livid at his unilateral decision; the evidence was as sparse as his efforts to discuss the matter with her. But just as he said then as he said anytime after that when it resurfaced. He said, "You should be grateful, mother. I discovered it before it happened." The fact that he had a supposed "sixth sense" was less than reassuring.

Now four years later and Tony's efforts had only made matters worse. Morale was low. Production was low, and sales were in the toilet; the fact that they were able to keep the lights on was a miracle; a miracle that came out of her life-savings. But Tony would not be told what to do. He was certain his path was right; he insisted that he was a gift to the company, that instead of scolding he should be praised and promoted further. He asserted that any lost money was simply "the cost of doing business;" not one to lose he always spun reality to his favor.

As he put the spotlight on him, Barb despaired, watching her company sink even further. Although head of the Finance Department there seemed little she could do to curtail his ambitions; arguing with him was as exhausting as trying to keep her company afloat; with every month she watched her savings dwindle, and yet he blamed everyone but himself.

Despite averaging $2.6 million the last fifteen years, and enduring repeat recessions, the company had managed to not fire a single employee. Tony changed all that. He saw his parent's commitment to their employees as cowardliness; the only path to success was by cutting the anchor, and at once he began purging, believing it was the employees holding the company back; he fired without first training anyone new, which consequently left huge gaps in expertise, product knowledge, and experience.

But Tony was convinced he had all the answers; he often stated he was gifted with divine powers, giving him the brilliance to lead, and who better to ignite a renaissance than he; but if anyone thought that implied responsibility they were poorly mistaken. There were two words Tony did not have in his vocabulary: responsibility and accountability.

He cut the life support systems of the company, simply expecting others to follow behind and solve the problems; he liked to say he was a professional problem solver, but in reality he was a professional problem starter. He was anything but a grand strategist.

And this was why Barb met with Arthur. She needed him to solve the problems, not to follow her son necessarily, but to do what her son could not; though lacking in experience, he was respectful, imaginative, but most importantly modest. He shouldered responsibility and owned his decisions, which won him immediate respect from others in the company; he was in many ways a liaison between the top and the bottom of the company, and if anyone could pull it off it was he. She believed it; moreover, he was not pompous or egotistical.

"My son will be the death of this company," she said to him, resigning to that sad fact. Hope crossed her face. "But before that happens maybe you can help me realize my dream."

"What's that," he asked.

"Grow this company beyond three million."

Chapter 2

Exploitation

While Tony embraced his mother's dream he saw it much differently than she did. He too wanted the company to grow, but only if he was in charge. There was nothing more that he wanted in the world than to be CEO.

"We have to live it and own it," he often said, introducing new policies as quickly as he changed them; those that failed to keep pace he fired. Not surprisingly, anxiety rose steeply, with employees fearing for their job on a daily basis. "When people are kept on their toes they perform better."

Barb disagreed and argued with him daily, insisting what he needed was a woman in his life. It wasn't that he was single. It was that he was gay, but it wasn't his homosexuality that bothered her. It was his egotism that played into it. Tony loved attention. Even his coming out had been done in front of a crowd of thousands of people during a rally. She accepted his lifestyle, but she loathed his leeching. "He is a parasite," she said, cursing him. "He needs someone to check him and keep him balanced."

His ambitions knew no end, and he was willing to be gay if it meant capitalizing on a social issue; this seemed preposterous except that Tony admitted it time and again. He loved to bask in the limelight; he fervently rejected the notion that homosexuality was linked to genetics, insisting instead that it was the best way to get a dog to lick his bone. He treated his dates like inferiors, second-class citizens, or even slaves, as he obliged them to refer to him as master.

"There is not one part of him that is gay," she said. "I raised him. I *know* every part of him."

And Tony was the first to admit it. "Guys are just easier to work with," he said, happily admitting the truth. "I can tell them what to do, and they'll do it for me if they want a treat. It's a lot like raising dogs." To him, it was just easier to peruse gay bars for fellatio and future candidates for the company; he imagined an army of subservient gay men following his vision. He frequently admitted to jerking off to that idea as well as the male employees at the office; the idea that one could leverage blowjobs for job security was his idea of brilliance.

Chapter 3

Serving the Entitled

Tony often spoke to Arthur about his vision of the future. He spoke of having a conglomerate of many companies. "You will run everything while I put my feet on the desk," he said, smiling happily.

* * * * * * * *

Arthur's first task was resolving company morale. Not surprisingly, Tony's purges were extremely unpopular; the fact that he reminded staff daily of the fragility of their job did him no favors. And for whatever reason, he thought it was a smart idea to flaunt his salary. It was $80,000, which by some standards was small, but the fact that it was his first job ever infuriated others; he had never worked a minimal wage job in his life.

Moreover, he added in commissions and gave himself a bonus, which further dragged morale down; the fact that he reminded employees that they worked so that he could relax was enough to throw in the towel. "I just want everyone to know," he said making an unexpected public service announcement, "that everyone here works hard so that I can make- one day- $750,000. That is the goal we share together."

What others took as demoralizing he took as spectacular; he believed he could write the next bestseller on inspiring leadership, "We cannot grow our business if we don't know how we're going to do, and we have to systemically do the same thing every month, and remember the top is always served first." Who else but him thought those were words of inspiration.

Often he unwarrantedly advised Arthur, "You have to give people goals," he said, feeling blessed that he was so wise. His smiles were disturbing; his words were as repulsive as they were patronizing, and too often he felt inclined to remind others of their place "Being at the bottom only means you can greater serve those on top."

Somehow he believed his words were moving, almost religious. He felt that when he spoke the winds shifted course; he felt the sun pour down upon him and he felt elevated as if levitating; he once compared himself to Jesus and said the only difference between them was that Jesus wished he was as great. Perhaps it was no surprise that his words were often followed by long silence instead of applause.

He reminded others that he going to be CEO one day, dipping morale to such levels that it seemed impossible to ever recover. "I have to say it's so nice to know that you'll be taking orders from me one day."

One of his policies required employees to greet him every morning. When Arthur failed to greet him he went berserk. "We are a team," he said, having a temper tantrum. "Welcoming one another is just as important as respecting the chain of command!"

"So greet me and then I'll greet you."

"I will as soon as you greet me. That's how the world works around here!"

Chapter 4

A Promising Future

In six years, Tony purged 60 employees. He masturbated nearly every night to the thought of it.

* * * * * * * *

As soon as Sallie and Arthur began dating, Tony began envisaging him as his future operations manager. Pulling him aside, he tried to fill his head with lavish ideas of success, wealth and cars, and even played on his desire to travel abroad; Tony assured him of all this and more, promising him a bright future if only Arthur would submit to his will, serving him faithfully and doing his bidding without question. But as charismatic as he was Arthur had his reservations. After all, Tony's words rarely matched his deeds.

13

In addition to his failures, arrogance, and repeated business blunders he also tiptoed a dangerous line when he redefined the meaning of "equal opportunity employment," viewing everyone as equal *beneath* him: he "permitted" employees to spend their lunch moving his new and very expensive desk into his office- as if they had a choice. And as a proponent of gender equality, he "allowed" female staff to haul in his heavy file cabinet without bothering to help.

More disconcerting, however, was his invitation for Arthur to attend his therapy sessions. There he learned that Tony was manic bipolar. Although medicated, Tony felt it held him back and admitted to not taking it; after three sessions, it became apparent that all Tony was interested in talking about was becoming CEO. He evaded questions about his medication, his feelings, or how his actions might affect others. Instead, he constantly returned to the discussing his future; he wanted someone to run the company, to build it up and expand it, and do all detail work while he acted as the company's "ambassador."

"I am the face of this company," he said.

"So your parents have passed the torch."

"They will."

"They haven't yet?" asked the therapist, and that was the end of the session. Tony got a new therapist. He resented being challenged. He wanted cheerleaders, yes-men, and loathed anyone that reminded him of his current disposition; his mind was always on the future never the present. When he networked and shook hands he always introduced himself as the future CEO of the company; when his parents learned of this he apologized for nothing, feeling he had every the right to say it.

He felt entitled to the lights, cameras and center stage. He took all the credit for his father's reputation, the company's growth, and was amazed that nobody wanted to step into his shadow; when he issued directions they were as vague as his vision. He had never taken orders, believing such an act was beneath him. "Every order I give should be carried out exactly as I envision it," he said to one manager. "Even if I only give vague instruction it should be perfect." Tony had a habit of expecting others to read his mind.

He told his therapists how frustrated he was with his mother, how she should just retire, and how restricted he felt with her still employed; he cursed her as if she were a stranger that had just rear-ended him. He admonished her efforts to direct his creativity; what she considered to be productive he viewed as unimaginative; he was not content with learning from his elders. He wanted to lead, to drive, to push new frontiers, believing that was the future of the company. "No pain, no gain," he said. And if Barb was unwilling to accept that fact then something would have to be done about it.

"My mother doesn't see my potential," he said to his new therapist. This was his sixth one. "What I need is for her to see my potential and just let me take the reins."

"Have you tried showing her your talents?"

He gave the therapist a look. "My mother doesn't need to see my talents. She just needs to step down."

Chapter 5

The Purges

On Election Day, Tony ordered on threat of termination that everyone was to wear a button or shirt in support of his presidential pick, Barack Obama. When Barb hastily tried to intervene for fear of lawsuit he threw up his hand to stop her, alleging that she had no right to infringe upon his 1st Amendment.

* * * * * * * *

Arthur was just as disturbed by Tony's conceited attitude as Barb was; he had fired yet another sales agent, and as sales shrank he refused to be blamed for it. Instead, he pointed right back at his mother, accusing her of having hired the wrong people in the first place. "I'm just cleaning

17

up your mess." Barb tried to interject but was cut off; there was no stopping Tony or his purges. Left and right, he pointed his fingers like a gunslinger and emptied desks.

"Bang, you're gone."

"Bang, see ya later."

"Bang, you're history."

The more Barb protested the more employees were walked out the door. She ordered to him to stop but he was having too much fun undermining her; he purged until he felt all the "deficiencies" had been removed. Finally, she threatened to fire him. He burst out in laughter.

"You can't fire me, mother. I'm your son!"

<u>Chapter 6</u>

Employee Appreciation Day

"When I'm CEO," he told Arthur, as if gazing into a crystal ball. "I will need somebody that can run all thirteen of my companies." At the rate he was going there wouldn't even be a headquarters left.

* * * * * * * *

For over thirty years, Employee Appreciation Day had honored the loyalty and dedication of the company's employees. Tony instead saw it as an opportunity to bolster his position as heir apparent as well as propagate his vision for growing the company; not surprising, few if any shared his optimism or his opinion. Morale was abysmal and production was only holding out of fear of termination;

nevertheless, Tony had everyone applaud him for "cutting away the fat." It was the weakest applause in history.

In his delusions, he saw everyone reaching for the skies; he saw thousands of fans cheering him on, and felt what he was doing was right. "As your sales manager, my job is to help this company grow. So, I want to remind each of you to get out there and make this company strong." He saw smiles where frowns existed; there was not one person that didn't express their resentment of him.

And on this day, a day meant for employees, Tony spoke for over an hour, lauding his vision, and happily reminded staff of their place beneath him. By the time he finished everyone got stuck in traffic. This created a long day of customer complaints and increasingly bitter hatred towards him. Employee Appreciation Day was meant to be about the employees. It used to be fun, but no longer. Now it was painful, artic cold to their efforts, and as repulsive as vinegar; in the past there used to be a barbeque, games and even cold beer. It was an all-day thank-you. Now it started at 6 AM, there were only coffee and donuts, and it was just Tony talking about how great he was.

Chapter 7

Sabotage

Employee Appreciation Day was also the day when the Employee of the Year was awarded. Nominees were taken all year long and placed in a box for safekeeping. Since Tony had moved the box into his office it came as no surprise that he won every year.

* * * * * * * *

Barb had every right to be worried. She was about to lose her company, and it all fell on Tony. And yet, he refused to accept any blame. "Everybody should want to grow," he told her. And yet, after three years none of his visionary ideas had caught on; the only thing that had was people flying out the door. If employees weren't fired then they quit.

But Tony was unperturbed. He continued about as usual, networking, selling, losing money and sending out emails with his title as CEO. He solicited advice from other business owners to ask them about their growth strategies; he then misinterpreted those strategies. In one instance, a CEO told him to hire only the best, which he took to mean purging some more. He gave two employees thirty days to learn a new language. Then he overworked them. "There's exceptional people, and then there's you," he told them.

He ordered a sales agent to shadow him for the month and then fired him at the end because the man had no sales to report; but how could he if he was shadowing him? Tony didn't see it that way. He claimed the man had poor performance. He also dismissed the human resources manager, who had become overwhelmed from his purges. "We are a company dedicated to growth, and you are an anchor holding us down."

Chapter 8

Bad Advice

Tony fired an employee for insubordination when the man forgot to bring him a pen.

* * * * * * * *

Among the advice he received from CEOs, Tony was encouraged to seize the day, which he once again misinterpreted to mean purging, but this time he went after his parents; enough was enough. "I need to secure my destiny," he said to Arthur, calling him up unexpectedly and asking for his help in his coup. Arthur, taken aback by it, was not surprisingly reserved.

"I don't think that's a good idea."

"Listen, this is going to happen," he said. "I'm going to fire my mother, and my father, and even my sister. I need you with me on this. So, are you with me?"

Arthur had no words. Too stunned to say anything, he couldn't believe anybody would ever wish to do a thing like this; he learned later Tony had altogether stopped taking his medication.

"I still don't think it's a good idea."

"It is what it is," he replied, insistently. This was going to happen, and in his mind he was giving Arthur a chance to profit from it.

"I can't see any reason behind this."

"Then you're not as astute as I am. There's way too much chaos at the company. I need to repair it just like I need to repair my family," he said softly. "I know that by firing my family I will heal the wounds and help bring us back together." Apparently, he believed his actions had only benefited the company, including the purges; he saw no wrong in anything he had done. According to Tony the rift in his family was entirely owed to the decline at the office, which was a result of poor management, bad employees, and a directionless company.

"I need to restore my parent's company, and the only way I can do that is by firing my parents and removing my sister. It's the only way, and I know that they'll under-stand. I need to salvage what's left of my inheritance."

But it was undoubtedly clear he was living in a fantasy world. His every decision had cost hundreds of thousands of dollars; his purges had caused irrevocable damages, personal as well as financial; morale was at an all-time low; production was holding, but the bare minimum was all the company was getting; employees were either quitting or working on their résumés at lunch. The company was on the brink of shutting his doors, but somehow Tony refused to accept any responsibility; his seemingly popularity was imploding the company.

But Tony continued to believe in his vision, advancing its credibility as though it was the answer to the company's woes; he propagated it everyday, preaching it like religion and converting followers by force if necessary; he denied any wrongdoing and when management finally had had it and protested he purged them too. Now all at once there were large gaps in the chain of command, but Tony simply inserted himself and assumed control.

"There is nobody more talented than I," he said, directing multiple departments; more résumés went out.

Barb insisted that those vacancies be filled, but Tony refused. Why pay somebody when he could do the job?

"But you don't do any work," she said, irate.

He dismissed that as ridiculous. Then he put his feet on the desk and relished being the sole person each department had to speak with; he issued vague directions that often led to mistakes. He accepted no responsibility; when departments complained he just pointed the finger. He wasn't interested in being responsible or accountable. He just wanted the titles; if it was chaotic before it was madness now.

The only department outside his grasp remained finance, and Tony tried everything imaginable to interject; he dreamed of controlling the money, because whoever controlled the cash of the company controlled the company itself, and he believed he was entitled to spend frivolously.

At first he tried sermonizing, believing that his vision would win over Barb's team. It didn't. She had a firm hold over her department; for whatever reason the former account manager had not been in the Finance Department, but rather had reported to the general manager that oversaw the day-to-day operations, a department that Tony was now nominally in charge of.

Unable to breech the walls with his preaching he resorted to underhanded tactics. He dismissed every helper in the warehouse just so he could hire more, set their pay, and then fire them later. This created a piercing migraine for accounts payable that struggled to keep up; he over-worked staff as well as team managers, elevating their stress and anxiety, forcing more people to quit and thus opening the doors for new hires; so long as he controlled the hiring process he had a foot in the door with the Finance Department; nearly every employee he fired was told he or she had performed poorly.

"People should want to strive forward," he said, uncaringly. "And I'm afraid this is no place for failures."

He then went a step further to force his foot in more and fired the last remaining sales agent; again, he alleged poor performance. Now there were almost no sales coming in.

<u>Chapter 9</u>

Meeting CEOs

And so Arthur was now faced with a choice. Should he agree to help Tony or not? In short, Tony was asking was the coup de grâce of absurdity, because nothing good was certain to come of it; it was no secret he just wanted to be CEO; he had no interest in managing, being held accountable to his actions or decisions. He simply wanted to be the face of the company and spend money like it was flowing from a never-ending fountain.

But of all the reasons the most pressing for why it was a bad idea was because he was dating Sallie; it was asinine to expect she would continue to date him if he agreed. Who would! Had Tony thought about that? More than likely he hadn't; moreover, did he really think his sister would be fond of the idea of being fired by her big brother?

So Arthur offered him an alternative instead. He offered to help him rebuild the company if he promised to never mention such an idea again. Tony considered it. To him it must have sounded like Arthur was agreeing to be his right-hand man; what else could it have meant? Arthur wasn't in fact saying that, but as long as Tony believed it he played along.

In the weeks that followed the two networked together, built business connections, developed sales goals (which Arthur pitched and Tony took the credit for) and began to rebuild the sales team; Arthur didn't care so much that Tony was taking the credit, so long as there was a company he could work for, get a paycheck, and pay off his student loans; if he married Sallie then there was even a future for him as a leader in the company. So, he didn't mind that Tony was taking the credit. He had his own personal stake for investing his time.

And Tony couldn't be happier. Everything Arthur did he claimed was his idea, his inspiration, and his flawless leadership. He introduced him at networking events as his right hand, exhibiting him like a showcase piece and going so far as to say he was "perfectly engineered to follow." Arthur didn't care; he couldn't afford to let it bother him anyway as there was so much to get done.

But others saw and knew the truth. The harder Arthur worked the more staff noticed; he stayed late at the office and came in early, sometimes he was the first one; he took on various roles from sales to project management; he kept lines of communication open, being as transparent as possible, and shouldering as much weight as possible; he helped out others by taking on issues and resolving them quickly; he multi-tasked, going far above and beyond what his job description entailed, setting standards that had rarely been seen.

And while Tony initially basked in the limelight of Arthur's efforts it wasn't to last; bit-by-bit the credit went to Arthur. Although he didn't ask for it others gave it to him. After all, he certainly had earned it; in sharp contrast, he worked for his reputation while Tony simply felt entitled to it. Not surprisingly, this created resentment, and all at once they began to clash; Tony wanted all the credit and would not settle for anything less.

At once he began to undermine Arthur, just as he had with his mother; the fact that this undercut his image was utterly lost on him. He demanded Arthur credit him publicly, acknowledging that it was his inspiration that both planted the idea and its execution; he set the terms. Arthur was to praise him religiously, laud his talents, and mention him only in the highest regards; a single act of neglect would be grounds for termination; whenever he referred to Arthur as the company's future operations manager it was meant to be buttressed with Arthur hailing him as a natural born leader; Arthur was to know his place, remember it, and never forget it. But unfortunately for Tony, the company's employees didn't agree. Neither did any of the company's business contacts. One CEO publicly praised Arthur after getting wind of his efforts.

"I hear you're doing in six months what my most senior employee does in ten years," he said, raising his glass. They were at a networking event. "Now you be careful, or I might just steal you away." Tony seethed with anger.

Chapter 10

Walking on Clouds

Immediately, Tony pulled Arthur aside, berating him for allowing a CEO to speak to him in such a way; how dare Arthur accept any form of compliment when clearly the credit was owed to him! Right then and there he reminded him of his place and what he expected of him.

"CEOs don't work for companies. Companies work for CEOs, and one day I will be a CEO. Just remember that!"

A few days later, they visited an acquaintance of Tony, who was so far into the clouds that he didn't know where Earth was anymore; he had ousted his parents, taken over the family business, and now recklessly fired and hired as he saw fit. He glorified himself, venerating his actions as morally necessary. "I had to save my inheritance," he told them. Tony couldn't agree more; who could argue with such an ethical philosophy? "It was either my family or the business, and in this world there's only one person that matters most, you."

Arthur was ready to go. He had heard enough. This CEO was not even thirty years old and was running a $25,000,000 company like a kid waving a loaded gun; he boasted about how many people he had fired; he said he had hired his parents under strict condition that they obey his every direction, including addressing him formally with a Mr. and his last name! It was utterly ridiculous.

Even more insulting was his executive office that resembled a college dorm more than a business room. "I have a flurry of ideas," he said, suddenly jumping onto his treadmill and dashing into a sprint. "This way I can get a good workout while I'm growing my business." In front of the treadmill were three monitors and a keyboard, so he could type while running; his earpiece was nearby so he could talk while running. Behind the monitors were two 72" plasma TVs so he could watch while talking, typing and running. In the corner of the room were a drum set and a mattress for his quick catnaps; he told them he only slept at most two hours a night; he owned a home, but was never there. When he ordered takeout he was still running, typing or talking on the phone. He never stopped.

"Don't ever let anyone slow you down," he said, alleging that anyone who couldn't keep pace didn't deserve to be employed. "In this world you're either running ahead or falling behind. And remember, failure is always someone else's fault, even if you stop to catch your breath."

Arthur had had enough. But then they went to another acquaintance that was more grotesque. Again, this CEO also seized his parent's three million dollar business and catapulted it to fifteen in less than five years; but that was only half of the story. The other half was that he bankrupted it; he liked to refer to himself as a start-up guru, which advertised economic brilliance but lacked sympathy for the wellbeing of the worker; he cared as much for the lives he destroyed as he did about the way he treated his parents, unremorseful. "They complained, but I put them in a senior home. It's better for them and me."

He entertained Tony's fantasy of being a landlord, of being a CEO, and doing what he loved without fear of consequence. "It's like I tell my accountant. If the IRS came to my door I'd remind them just who pays them and who keeps this country running. I do, so if they want any money from me, which they should be glad to get a penny then they'll do my bidding. It's like I always say, the world exists so that I can do what I love."

Arthur's jaw dropped. How could anyone be so pigheaded, so aloof to the hard efforts of the worker? It didn't mean Arthur was a socialist or communist, but he certainly believed in the worker as the foundation of a business, but apparently that was misguided; somehow a capitalist was to ignore the worker, take credit for everything, assume no responsibility or accountability, and blame others when things failed. If that was capitalism he was ashamed; his upbringing had taught him to respect those that made everything possible; in high school he had been part of the theater crew, acting behind the scenes to make the show possible, and it had amazed him even then how many actors were too much a prima donna to even clap for them at the end of a show.

But to make things worse, Arthur had noticed that while meeting both of Tony's acquaintances he had been largely ignored like a ghost, as though he was not even in the same room; even when they spoke about him they pretended like he wasn't there.

"I really envy you," said the CEO stepping off his treadmill. "I wish I had as good an operations manager as you do." They were talking about Arthur who was all of three feet away in the circle, but he might as well have been a mile away. "That's what leaders like us need. We need exceptional people who know exactly what we're thinking and get it done. That's what visionaries like us need."

Chapter 11

Vacations

With sales in sharp decline Tony thought it was a brilliant time to go to Europe.

But Barb refused. "Absolutely not. If you want to be this company's sales manager then do your job!

"I'm not asking for your permission, mother."

"Then maybe you won't have a job when you get back. I need sales not an employee who wants to do as he pleases whenever he wishes."

"This is a-once-in-a-lifetime opportunity. Now why would you deny that to me?"

She folded her arms. "How long do you expect to be gone?" She didn't want to capitulate, but she also didn't want to deny her child the opportunity to see the world.

"Two weeks."

"Two weeks! Forget it."

"Like I said, I'm not asking your permission. I'm just telling you."

"And what about sales?"

He gave her a sharp look. "Come on, this company was here before I was even born. I doubt it's going anywhere in two weeks."

Two weeks later, he called a companywide meeting to announce he was going on yet another trip; Barb objected loudly in front of everyone, but he stopped her.

"Everyone here works so I can go on these trips."

"Are you serious," she said dumbfounded; she couldn't believe he had the audacity to say something like that. "Do you think money just grows on trees? Do you think that's what our purpose here is, to let you see the world while we work?"

"You're the owner, mother. If you don't go then I will. That's what being the future CEO means."

She dropped her jaw. "You're no longer my sales manager. I will find someone else to replace you! If you want to go then go, but I don't work hard so you can just fly to wherever you want."

Tony only laughed aloud and two weeks later he returned from his trip in the Caribbean, relaxed and tanned.

"That was hard work," he said handing Barb all of his receipts.

"What's this?"

"Um, they're called receipts."

"Why are you giving them to me?"

"Because you're going to reimburse me."

"Like hell I am. You went on vacation."

Tony shook his head, rejecting that. "Who said I was on vacation? I was never on vacation."

"Yes you were."

"Did I say they were when I left?"

"It doesn't matter. I'm not reimbursing you."

"Well, you're going to because I networked for this company everyday, so unless you want to hear from the Department of Labor you will pay me back."

"Networked? How, by drinking alcohol and eating a expensive restaurants?"

"I network with everyone I meet."

"Even the waiter who served you?"

"Absolutely. It's all about who knows who."

She threw the receipts on the floor. "Get out of my office."

"Not before I see you enter the receipts."

"Then pick them up."

"I wasn't the one who knocked them off the desk," he said, increasing her agitation.

"Just because you talked with somebody doesn't mean these are business expenses," she said.

His calm but needling tone only angered her more. "Actually yes. As long as I have just five minutes of talking business I can write off the entire trip."

"Bullshit!"

But according to Tony and his brilliant knowledge of the Internal Revenue System he was right; it's what his acquaintances had told him, and it's what he believed to be true; after all, the IRS would undoubtedly agree since he was a future CEO and in a class separate from reality. After a long and belligerent argument she capitulated. A whole month of vacation had suddenly become business trips; and that set the precedent. From then on, he spent frivolously with the company's credit card, using it for personal matters and always alleging he was networking.

He began to fly regularly across the country, spending weekends with college friends, and accruing such incredible costs that his mother and sister had to give up their weekends to find ways to pay for it; he even justified dating and his frequent one-night stands as business related.

"You never know who you're going to meet at a bar or club." He submitted reimbursement for buying condoms.

Barb tried in vain to argue, but lost every time. Somehow her son always found a way to shift the facts in his favor; he spun reality to how he saw fit, spending far more money than he made, and neither apologized for it nor expressed regret; and this was just the beginning. All at once, he announced he was going on vacation.

"Mother, I've earned it. I'm exhausted from all this networking. So, I need a break."

"Are you serious!"

"Um, yes. I've been working nonstop, flying back and forth across this country and everywhere in the world. I deserve a bit of a break! You can't deny that to me. It's in the company handbook. I'm entitled to a certain amount of vacation days."

"You've already taken a vacation. You've had more than anyone in this company has ever taken."

"Mother, how many times do I have to tell you? I was networking. That's how businesses grow."

"But you're the sales manager! That's your job, not to fly around and meet people."

"No that's exactly my job! I'm generating leads."

"How is a lead across the country going to help us? How? Tell me how? We are a local business, so you tell me how you expect us to pay all the costs of doing a job halfway across the country?"

"That's not for me to figure out. I'm the sales manager, not the operations manager." He pointed to Arthur. "If you want those answers go to him, and if he doesn't have the answers then maybe he should be fired!"

All at once, she saw through him. This was all about Arthur; all of these trips were meant to divert credit back to Tony. He was trying to overwhelm Arthur, have him quit or get fired and then resume the credit he felt he was due. Suddenly, she went berserk. "He's done more for this company than you have flying around. Start doing your job and make me some money instead of just spending it!"

"I am doing my job, but if you have problems paying the bills then maybe you and dad need to consider the people you hire." Barb had hired Arthur, and it was if not the most resented fact that crawled on Tony's skin. "I'm doing my job of being the visionary for this company, but if you've got a problem with sales then you and dad need to ask yourself why this company is failing!"

Chapter 12

The Family Silver

In one year, Tony took off over four months and the company paid for everything.

* * * * * * * *

Barb resented ever giving birth to him. She pulled out her hair, and put his picture down on her desk; he was no son of hers. Then she took out a box of pencils and broke each one. She couldn't stand him; Arthur was seated across from her, saying nothing, just letting her vent. It was all she could do.

"I'm sorry," she finally said. "He just irritates the hell out of me."

He nodded. As much as he wanted to outright agree he was nevertheless tactful; blood was thicker than

43

water. "Perhaps he would be better in another role," he suggested.

"Why, do you want his job?"

Arthur chuckled. He knew Barb would hand it to him in a heartbeat; they had discussed it many times. But he felt it would only disrupt matters further; not only would Tony refuse to acknowledge Arthur as the new sales manager he would outright refuse to give up the title.

"If you want it it's yours."

"I just think there is a better way."

"So what are you suggesting," she asked.

"Well, he's good at marketing. Why not that?"

"He won't agree to just that." That was true.

"Unless, he's given a title with it," he said with a smirk; wily and clever. She liked that idea.

"Even still. He might refuse."

"That's entirely possible," he said. "So, it leaves two choices. Either let him have both titles or you decide for him."

She shifted in her chair. The thought made her uneasy; arguing with Tony was always unpleasant, but the very idea of letting him have his way was exasperating. It wasn't an easy choice.

"Either way," he said, "he already believes he runs this company."

She cast him a surprise look. "What do you mean? How does he believe he runs this company?"

"Well, he puts CEO in his emails." He thought she was aware of this. She wasn't.

"Do you know this for sure?"

"Of course, I have access to his email."

She looked even more surprised. "Wait, how do you have access to his email?"

"Because he gave me his login and password. He said he wanted me to sort through his mailbox.

"Like a secretary? He wants you to be his secretary. Un uh! I don't approve of that at all."

"I completely agree."

"He doesn't need a secretary to sort through his email. He needs to get his life together and do his job. That's what he needs to be doing."

"I couldn't agree more," he said, strengthening his alliance; blood was indeed thicker than water, but there was a chance to turn things around. He had strong feelings for Sallie, and if this as indeed to be his future then he wanted to ensure it as much as possible, and if that meant isolating

Tony then so be it; as Arthur saw it, containing him was critical to the growth of the company.

"So, it will be a promotion for him then?"

"A promotion? Why a promotion," she asked.

"Because he won't take it any other way."

That was also true.

Barb sighed. The thought of "promoting" her son was grotesque, but she couldn't fire him; she had failed to follow through in removing him as sales manager, so what options did she have left?

Chapter 13

Minimum Wage

Tony accepted the "promotion" of Marketing Director, but as predicted retained his current role as sales manager. He refused to give it up. After all, he wanted smart peons, not leaders.

* * * * * * * *

Although the two were close in age, Arthur differed from Tony in nearly every aspect; from the way they treated others to how they strategized, neither shared any similarity. Whereas Arthur had earned minimum wage in the past, Tony's first job was being the heir apparent. Whatever he wanted, he got, even his choice of college was agreed to after much debate; he wanted not just the prestige, but also selected one of the most expensive institutions in the nation.

Although he frequently alleged he had worked in the past his internships could hardly be counted. "I've had two marketing jobs before I came here," he once said to Arthur, but the fact was he had done nothing more than swivel in a chair, spewing out ideas. Unlike Arthur, he had neither worked a minimum wage job in his life nor felt the need; whatever humility was gained from minimum wage was lost on him. As such, he lacked any respect for those who performed the hard work.

This sharply differed from Arthur, who had in fact sweated for minimum wage; so desperate had he been for a job that he pursued a minimum-wage job 11 times before finally getting it. He wasn't born into wealth, at least not like Tony; while money is relative, and he was certainly better off than others his upbringing taught him the value of money as well as how to respect it; there were many nights that he ate tuna straight out of a can. But no matter what he learned to adapt, bending to the wind in order to succeed in life.

Tony was the total opposite. He callously ignored the pain or struggle of others, insisting that his life was more important than theirs; his placed his vision on a pedestal, coercing others to worship it. He viewed himself as a blessing, a protégé of perfection; he had neither suffered hardship nor knew its meaning and yet felt he knew exactly how to cure it. "Those people that can't do things simply haven't strived enough."

He saw others as followers; admirers of his, even if they didn't know it already. He molded himself as a savior, his persona lionized for all to feel his glory; if people weren't worshipping him it was only because they were being distracted; who wouldn't want to worship him? He was an evangelist, rarely practicing what he preached; he was prophet for profit, and his humility only knew how to coax new followers, to sucker them in.

Arthur won admiration, not from false imagery, but from hard work. He modeled for others, setting the standard and holding himself accountable to every decision he made; he added responsibilities to his caseload and accepted failure as a teaching tool; when he fell he got right back up. He spoke with confidence, not to preach, but to assert that he knew what he was talking about; when others hesitated he marched ahead, gaining the respect of co-workers as well as clients and competitors.

He had loans like any college kid and was working hard to pay them off. But whereas Arthur's parents taught him the virtues of perseverance, persistence and the power to believe in himself, Tony simply felt entitled as though the world owed him. Insecure about his sexuality, he blamed his mother for not accepting his lifestyle, going so far as to publicly shame her. But therein lay the reason for her approval of Arthur and not Tony:

Both Victor and her had come from low working class homes, often teetering on poverty. Barb had had it the worst. She had lived among the rats and her family had made due with a small tenant apartment back in the old country. As a young woman she had worked for next to nothing, eating when she could, and starving most of the time. The first chance she got she came to America, where she met Victor. He too had come from abroad. They fell in love, married, and gave birth to two children. But never once did she forget her roots, for if anybody understood the value of money it was Barb; she wasn't great at finances but she certainly tried her best. She once admitted how badly she would do trying to sell lemonade. "But I'd still try," she said, taking pride in her determination.

And it was her experience with hardship that drew her closer to Arthur. She trusted him, giving him access to the database as well as her blessing for proposing the idea of marriage to Sallie. She appreciated him, and all he was doing for the company; he was trying to build a town around a goldmine whereas her son was roping it off.

"This is the land of opportunity," she said to Arthur. "But you got to make that opportunity for yourself. Nobody is going to give it to you." Of all the people she and Victor had ever interacted with, Arthur was the first to win their admiration so quickly.

Chapter 14

Going through Coaches

Through traveling, Tony met international CEOs, world delegates, and political leaders. When he received two humanitarian awards those from Europe, Asia, and the Middle East congratulated him.

* * * * * * * *

In addition to his negligence, Tony also expended huge amounts on trade shows, sponsorships, and furniture for new branch offices that he neither had nor had gotten his parent's blessing for; he stockpiled, filling the warehouse and argued with his father when he refused to move it. But then came the coaches, and the price tag of his vision soared through the roof.

"We need to come together as a team," he told his mother, taking the high moral ground. "Only by being on the same page can we see the vision ahead." Seeking affirmation, he hired coaches like someone buys greeting cards; if they failed to cheerlead his ideas he dropped them; if they failed to cheer loud enough he dropped them. They dangled like puppets on a string doing his bidding until either he grew tired of them or they just quit; in three years he went through five business coaches. One he dismissed publicly, right after the man presented his parent's with a plaque at the company's appreciation day. Somehow, Tony felt like he should have been the recipient.

Chapter 15

The Credo

At one particular annual Employee Appreciation Day, Tony had every employee write down on a piece of paper their hopes and dreams; several wished to send their children to college. He then ordered them to tear it in half, and put his vision of the company first and foremost.

* * * * * * * *

Believing that every decision of his was a stepping-stone towards growth, Tony conceived of a credo that neither added to his popularity nor was accepted. "I am building a change coalition," he proudly told Arthur when he had finished writing it. Making it mandatory at every meeting it began by him asking a question followed by the crowd's response:

"WHERE DO WE WANT TO GO?" he said, loudly cupping his mouth like a megaphone.

"2 more states," everyone replied, apathetically.

"HOW ARE WE GOING TO GET THERE?"

"Teamwork."

"WHAT IS THE BEST PLACE TO WORK?"

"Here," they said, denying it internally.

"AND WHO IS THE KING?"

"Cash." Which was just another name for Tony.

As difficult as it was to chant it was even harder to embrace. Three years of this bullshit was enough; his so-called vision had no more magic left. In the beginning, his charisma had stolen the show, and everyone was excited to see what might come about as a result of it, but after three hollow years it was just a birthday gift that nobody wanted.

Sadly, long after Arthur, he would still be pushing it, hiring new people who were naïve to its emptiness.

Chapter 16

Italian Food

Like everyone else, Barb hated the credo. Aside from personifying Tony's narcissism, which nobody needed a reminder of, it did nothing to promote morale; the faces of everyone were enough proof of that. But the fact that Tony then scheduled an Employment Appreciation Day on the same day as her birthday was just infuriating. Not only did she have to wake up an hour earlier than usual, but then she also had to jump right into his godforsaken credo and pretend like she gave a shit.

By the time the workday was over all she wanted to do was lay on her bed and watch TV, but Tony refused, insisting that everyone go out to eat. Yet, he rejected every place she proposed.

"But it's my birthday. I can go where I want."

"You can go there anytime, mom, but I know a great place that you're going to love."

"Maybe you didn't hear me. I want to go where I want to go! Why is this such a problem for you?"

"I'm just saying, you can go there anytime. But I do a lot of networking and going to dinners and I know a lot of great places to eat that are better than that one."

"I know you eat out a lot. On my dime! So tonight, we're eating where I want to eat."

But he didn't let up. Intolerably inflexible, he went back and forth with her for twenty minutes while everyone sat on the couch and waited.

"But I like the food! I like the music. I like that place, and that's where I want to go," she said, hammering in her wish. "If you want to go to your place then you go, but that's where I'm going!"

"But why settle, mom? There's better places."

"Oh my God," said Sallie, sick of listening to it. "Just let her go where she wants to go. It's not a big deal."

"All I'm saying is that she can go there anytime," he replied. "Why not try a new place. This is her birthday, and I know she will like it. It's a special place and I know she'll be glad we went."

His obstinacy was irritating. Victor tried to get a word in, but Tony refused to be silenced. He knew his pick was far superior to his mother's and he wanted her to have a great time; he considered picking a restaurant for her his birthday gift, and the fact that she was rejecting it was insulting to him.

After an hour and still hungry, Barb finally gave in. "Fine, let's go where you want. Clearly, I can't have my way on my birthday, so lead the way. Let's go. Everyone out the door!"

The food was superb and the atmosphere lively, but that didn't excuse Tony for his behavior; while Barb did enjoy herself she wasn't about to admit it. She remained bitter and hostile to him, particularly when he used the evening to network with other customers eating as well as the staff; she adamantly refused to write off the dinner as a business expense the next day.

"But why not," said Tony, dumbfounded. "It was a great night of networking."

"It was my birthday. That's why."

"That doesn't make any sense. It was a business dinner, so therefore it can be written off."

"It was my birthday, or at least it was supposed to be, but instead of my son letting me enjoy my one evening to have a pleasant time with my family he picked where I was to eat, then talked to every stranger in the place, and now wants me to write it off."

Tony didn't see what the problem was. He had enjoyed himself immensely, laughing, and basking in the limelight as he went around the tables, shaking hands as though he was the restaurant's manager; most mistook him for being it. "I was networking, and there is nothing wrong with that. I am the sales manager at this company, and if my job is to bring in sales then I need to generate leads, and there's nothing wrong with getting to know people, because you never know who needs our services."

"But you made me wear a ridiculous hat!"

"It was a steakhouse," he said, still trying to figure out why she was upset. "You can wear a cowboy hat at a steakhouse. There's nothing wrong with that. There's no law that says you can't do that."

"But it was my birthday!"

He refused to be shamed. "Yes, it was your birthday, but if you didn't have a good time then that's your fault. I wanted you to have a good time, because you're my mother and I love you. But I can't make you smile. That's up to you. If you choose to not have fun then that's your decision."

"But it was my birthday!"

"Well, I'm done discussing this," he said. "I'm sorry you had a shitty birthday. Perhaps you'll choose to have a better one next year."

Chapter 17

Catalogues

According to Tony, every idea of his was worth its weight in gold. So, Barb thought he should lock himself in a vault and lose the key.

* * * * * * * *

Believing in his brilliance he rejected everyone else's ideas except his own; he vetoed Sallie's, belittling them as childish and going so far as to shame her publicly.

"Your ideas are just not as great as mine," he said, neither caring to hear what she had to say nor offering to pool ideas in a brainstorm session; he had as much interest in sound-boarding ideas as he had for doing any work. "The only thing everyone needs to do is listen to me, and we will grow."

Taking the advice of his acquaintances, he blamed others for his mistakes, asserting that it was impossible for him to fail. When he negotiated a deal at $80,000 he lost nearly ten thousand of the profit; he had sold it for thirteen. Another time he alleged it was operations fault, but nothing could be further from the truth. In a third instance, he felt it was invaluable to open an account with a catalogue vender; he saw the money pouring in. Unfortunately, he neither considered the expense of the vender's catalogues nor the time commitment required to sell out of the catalogue; his shift of accountability and responsibility onto others meant they had to juggle extra duties in addition to their own.

But Tony always put the cart before the horse and he ignored the pain and suffering of others. It wasn't his problem that an employee couldn't do it all; anyone who couldn't do his or her job was purged; they protested, but that only resulted in more purges. But to make matters even worse- if that was even possible- the catalogues failed to generate any revenue; it was simply asking the impossible for an employee to shoulder the extra weight. Moreover, what did a receptionist know about salesmanship?

This isn't to suggest people can't learn new skills, but Tony neither trained his staff nor offered an ounce of encouragement; he simply expected. And not surprisingly, the results were deplorable; the cost of the catalogues far outweighed the sales. But to add insult to injury, Tony had customized the catalogues, adding to its cost. Thus, he had spent exorbitant amounts for hardly any return. In the end, the catalogues ended up on a shelf, collecting dust.

Chapter 18

Trade Shows

For someone who propagated going green, social media, and online marketing it made little sense why Tony ordered *paper* catalogues. But for whatever reason he lauded it as one of his most brilliant ideas.

* * * * * * * * *

In addition to his hefty expenditures, losing sales, and lofty sales ventures Tony also signed the company up for a dozen tradeshows that proved to be neither relevant nor profitable; he signed up the company and wasted over two hundred hours selling to markets outside of the company's specialty; it puzzled the employees that had to give up their day as it did for the people at the tradeshows, who wondered why they were there.

"It's all about the synergy," said Tony, proudly spreading his evangelism in the hopes of converts. He had the company spend over ten thousand dollars on failed tradeshows.

But to his credit, Tony was passionate – though it was limited to being in front of the camera; he neither cared for the wellbeing of others, the company, or others. So long as he was applauded he was happy. His impetuous nature cost time and money; he ignored the details, focusing only on the bigger picture without any map to get there; his ideas erred; his finger-pointing incited resentment; he neither learned humility nor adapted to his environment. He simply required others assimilate to his entitlement: he once came upon a local charity event that was struggling. At once, he took it over, using his charisma to capture the imaginations of others. Within an hour the event was pulling in hundreds of people; to his credit he knew how to market, but only if everyone listened and did exactly what he said.

But while his talents were praised his weaknesses were revealed; he acted as a hub, where all trains came and left. The second he left the event it all unfolded: without any leadership the event collapsed; he had neither trained staff nor prepared them for such success; he far outpaced everyone else and they simply couldn't keep up. He later asked his mother to pay him for that weekend event,

because as he alleged, "I was practicing being a visionary."

Chapter 19

Leadership Meetings

In addition to buying furniture for his future branch offices he also leased three locations worth $25,000 each, but he neither had a business plan to expand and use them nor had his parent's approval. Thus, the company now owed $75,000 with nothing to show for it.

* * * * * * * * *

Despite Arthur's best efforts morale was still low, and at his suggestion Barb called an emergency meeting of the leadership team; it was time for Barb to intervene on behalf of the company. Tony had gone on long enough, and she needed to put her foot down once and for all.

Right away, Tony took over the meeting, treating everyone as though they were subordinate to him; he recited his list of demands, expecting that everyone was taking notes and prepared to do his bidding without question; he laid out his plans for expansion, volunteered his parent's approval, and demanded Sallie willingly forfeit her right as a future successor of the company. He was taken aback when he met resistance.

"Are you serious?" she said in disbelief. "Just who do you think you are? Of course I'm not going to just let you run the company!"

"I'm just doing what's best for the company."

"And you think you can do it alone?"

"I'm sorry you can't accept the facts," he said, arrogantly dismissing her opinion. "If you wanted to help run things you should show an interest, but all I see is you coming to work and going home. You don't further your education. You don't network. You don't even come up with ideas to help us grow as a company."

"That's because you don't listen!"

"Because your ideas are juvenile! They're inconsistent with how to grow a business; you don't read books, you don't talk to business owners like I do, and you don't spend any time developing your ideas. That's what I do. I've put forth the effort, but you haven't."

"According to you," she said, reaching out to strangle him. She wanted to squeeze the life out of him. "How can I possibly take the time to develop ideas to grow this company when you're out spending money and not bringing in sales. I spend my weekends at the office, trying to find a way to pay for everything while you're off joking around with friends on the company's dime."

"I'm generating leads."

She threw her arms up. "Then where are the sales from these leads?"

"It's not my job to turn them into sales. I generate leads and turn them over to others. If somebody else is dropping the ball then that's not my problem."

"But you're the sales manager!"

He shook his head. "I generate the leads only."

"Yeah, but why are you traveling across the country for leads when there's plenty right here?"

That was an excellent point, but as always Tony had an answer. "Because you never know who knows who; it's all about getting around the gatekeepers. I meet all sorts of people that know others that know CEOs, presidents, directors, and decision makers. I don't waste my time trying to get in the front door; that's what amateur salesmen do.

When I go to a client I already know who the decision maker is and I get right in."

"So why not do that here?"

"Because CEOs and presidents are mobile people. They don't necessarily live in the same place they work. I travel to meet these people, generate leads, and I do this to help grow this business." His answer was snobbish and did nothing to ingratiate the efforts of others.

"You're such an asshole!"

"I'm sorry you feel that way," he said, shaming her publicly. "I believe we need to be honest with one another. I do my part, but do you do yours?"

"Of course I do mine."

"Not when you spend you're weekends at the office instead of networking."

Had he not been listening? "Because I'm cleaning up your mess. That's why! What are you deaf?"

"That's not very professional."

"Fuck you!"

Despite the meeting being held in a public place it was still becoming loud. Tony was unsympathetic, abrasive, and dismissive; it was made worse by their father ignoring their feuding and watching the television; he ordered food and ignored them as best as possible. Thus, it was left up to Barb to do something.

"Listen, I want the three of you to run things after us," she said. But Tony disagreed. At once, he waved his finger in disapproval.

"That's very unwise. This company needs vision to take it to the next level, and neither of these two have that." His sister barked at that, but he kept going. "That may be harsh, but it is what it is. Mom, you and dad have done a great job bringing the company to this point, but now we need to take that next step and to do that requires something much more than what either of these two have; it requires inspiration. That's what I can do."

"Bullshit," Sallie said.

He ignored her. "Unlike my sister, I don't let my emotions get the better of me. This is a business meeting and I believe it is important to be professional."

"You're a fucking retard," she added. "You absolutely despicable."

"I'm trying to be realistic, and the fact is you're just better at taking directions than giving them."

Sallie stormed off, furious at him as well as her dad for not saying a word.

"What I'm saying may sound hurtful," he said, turning to Barb, "But it's important that everyone be able to recognize his or her strengths and weaknesses. Dad knows what his are. I know what mine are. She just needs to admit hers. I am the future of this company, and if that's not what she wants to hear then she can always work someplace else." His words were as poisonous as they were insulting.

"You should not speak to your sister that way," Barb said, trying to reprimand him.

"I only speak the truth, mom. I wouldn't be helping her grow if I coddled her. I want her to excel and if that means pushing her a bit- and in the process being honest by hurting her feelings- then that's what I'll do. I want only the best for her."

"But you don't need to say those things that way."

"It's the only way, mom. I need you and dad to realize that the only future this company has is through me, not from her or from him," he said, pointing to Arthur.

As Sallie came out of the bathroom from wiping her tears her brother again assailed her. This time insisting that she henceforth report to him directly instead of Barb.

"I'm not a secretary, especially not yours!"

"I didn't say that."

"But it's what you meant."

"If that's how you view it. I need your help Sallie," he said, trying to appeal to her sensitive side.

"No, what you need is help."

He sighed, as though she simply wasn't getting it. He was a visionary. What he needed was an army of drones that could read his mind. Why was it so hard for his sister to understand this? Why was it so difficult for her to see the value he brought to the company? "You know me best, which is why I need you to report to me directly, because you know how I think better than anyone; you can be my mental interpreter."

"If you want a secretary then hire one." The sad truth was that he had; he had hired a secretary over a sales-person or technician, believing that somehow a secretary was more valuable. Currently, he was on his fourth one. But that was besides the point to him, inconsequential. He just wanted his sister to report to him, whatever that took.

"All of my ideas move this company forward," he said, almost patronizingly, as if he alone was responsible for the production of ideas. "But what I need is somehow who can keep pace, who can provide me with an accurate report of the day's financial situation. Only then can I grow this company. Only then can we go in the right direction."

"The only direction you're taking us is down."

Barb interjected, hoping to steer the conversation in another direction. "Who said anything about growth? We can't grow when everyone at work is unhappy. The first thing we need to do is bolster morale."

"Mom, if people are unhappy then they should go. People need to find happiness, but even the Declaration of Independence says that it is a pursuit and nothing more."

"But we can try and make it so."

He shook his head. "Mom, if you want to waste time trying to get people to smile then you go ahead. I'm trying to grow this company. I don't have time to check on everyone's happiness. That's not my job."

"When employees aren't happy production suffers. I want morale back up."

"The people that need to go are let go. This is how you grow a company, mom. You cut away the fat so the rest can strengthen; you and dad hired people that only held you back. You're attacking me for something that really isn't my fault, but if it makes you feel better to think of me as the villain then so be it. I'm just trying to grow this company. Besides, I know deep down that you really want to grow this company, but in order for that to happen you need to come to terms with the fact that I will be in charge one day. Right now you're struggling with that, but it's going to happen. It's not a matter of if, but when."

"Exactly. But right now we're in charge, so start doing what we tell you!"

Chapter 20

Higher Education

Tony blasted the company all over social media, sharing with the world all the supposed fun things that the company was doing; his videos showed the company as a great place to work; he showed off the human side and extolled morale as the highest of any company; this was his solution to raising morale. Portray it as such and the problem is resolved. But calling something young doesn't make it so, and his magical fountain did nothing but force employees to smile on camera.

"You never advertise what you're selling," he said to Arthur, always lecturing his profound wisdom. "Instead, you engage yourself with the community, share stories, volunteer knowledge, be giving, and then people will be curious about what you're selling. That's how you grow a company. When you give yourself people embrace that."

But for someone who preached giving he received the spotlight more often. Tony had a Bachelor's Degree, but frequently asserted he also had a Master's Degree; it was proudly displayed on his wall. Yet, the advanced degree was nothing more than a certificate from a motivational speaker, an internationally renowned man who asked people why they do what they do; it was not a Master's Degree at all, but a course offered by the speaker. It was about life mastery. But since Tony was an interpreter of reality he felt that since the speaker's website advertised the course's fees using the word "tuition" that he therefore was earning a Master's Degree. As asinine as it sounded no amount of logic could persuade him otherwise.

And so, once again on the company's dime, he flew to an island in the Pacific Ocean, spent two weeks cleansing his body of toxins, engaged with CEOs and other people that could afford the expensive course and returned feeling renewed and energetic. Upon his return, he made it obligatory that everyone welcome him as a graduate while he proudly displayed his certificate.

Chapter 21

An Excellent Salesman

Despite the catalogues being shelved, he insisted that the company continue to pay for the subscription. When Barb refused, he accused her of being a "terrorist to his creativity."

* * * * * * * * *

After a string of failed leadership meetings, Barb cancelled all future meetings. Sallie was thrilled, but Victor didn't understand why, not that he did anything, or paid any attention to the drama. "You got to give him a chance," he said to his wife, publicly admitting his ignorance of the situation; he was as oblivious as it got. Despite hearing the drama he simply tuned it out.

When Tony purged the company, Victor thought people were just quitting. "Don't worry about it. If they want to go, then let them. I'll hire more," he had said to his wife and daughter at the time. He was useless.

But then that's who Victor was; he neither cared nor worried about it. "If you don't like it, then don't look at it," he said, reciting his mantra. It was the words he lived by; it separated him, but then there were advantages to that. At one networking event, instead of wearing a tie, he wore a shirt with hotdogs on it. If you don't like it don't look at it. He certainly stood out in the crowd, and that was how he earned new business. After all, who could forget that?

And that's who Victor was. He saw the world from one window and closed all the rest; he neither cared for drama nor politics; he neither resolved family discord nor expressed any sign of emotion other than impatience. He was passionate about his work, enjoyed humor, and rarely voiced his opinion unless it personally affected him.

An ironclad republican, he listened to talk radio, watched conservative shows on TV after work, and snored over commentary by liberals; whenever his son wished to talk politics he simply fell asleep, believing that was a softer way of telling someone to shut up.

A. Ruben

He was a man of distance, preferring to have an escape route in case people sought him out for answers that he didn't have; when clients had questions he delayed; when employees had questions he left the building; he was the man in charge, the hub of all decision-making, and yet he had no desire to fulfill the role. He ignored questions like he ignored drama. So when Tony fired the company's accountant, alleging embezzlement he took it on face value; when the general manager was also fired he accepted that too.

To him, it was better to live in the world of denial than face reality. He was an owner, but that didn't mean he had to like it. He was a technician first. It was how he had started his business- and it was a role he enjoyed. He sold well, but only because he knew the technical end; he neither wore a tie nor presented himself in a clean manner. He was always dressed in old, worn-out jeans and boots, often less presentable than his greased up technicians. But this was the image his clients knew and trusted; after all, the more greasy a technician the more he must know.

He was an owner, but not an executive. He had an office, but it was so filled from his hoarding that it was used as storage; he preferred the desk and steel chair next to the warehouse so he could speak with his technicians as they left for the day; he gave them last minute instructions, asked if they had any questions- he cared about them- and talked shop.

His hands were as filthy as his clothes, but he didn't mind; he often used his grease knife to cut apples, never bothering to clean it. He was a man of grease.

He neither believed in growing the company nor investing in it, unless it aided his technicians, which he saw as the heart of the company; he refused to spend money on office equipment, opting instead to use twenty-five year old obsolete computers; he neither knew what a floppy disk was nor a flash drive, or the cloud. He thought the Internet was a subscription the company had like a magazine.

He wrote his proposals on paper and his brother, Antonio, faxed them. Where one was an obsolete dinosaur the other was a broken record, trying to get his brother to catch up with the times.

"I'll catch up later," Victor would always say, never doing it. He procrastinated as often as he hoarded, and the warehouse- what space there was- was consumed by his unproductive habit. Antonio tried to help his brother with technology, but in utter vain; Victor was an old dog, and it was simply easier to let him carry on, as he knew best.

If Victor showed any emotion whatsoever it was impatience. Otherwise, he was impartial. If Antonio forgot something Victor got upset; if others erred he got annoyed; he wasn't as insistent that others read his mind like his son, but he certainly had little patience when it came to the little things. But then that was simply a byproduct of his evasion. For instance, he got impatient when product wasn't ordered, but then how could it be when he still had to measure, and he hadn't measured because he had been ignoring the client's shouting, and the client was only shouting because he had procrastinated.

And this was how the company ran. Victor was the hub of all decision-making except financial. He was a notorious procrastinator, and ignored other's questions or problems unless he wanted to hear them; he neither guided his son nor shared his wisdom, finding meaning in the phrase, power is knowledge. And perhaps that is why his son wished to be the hub; he wanted to mirror his father.

While Tony sought the torch, doing whatever it took to get it, Victor was apathetic. He was simply more concerned about retiring than what his son was doing.

Chapter 22

Hitting a Nerve

With retirement on his mind, Victor was oblivious to all else but that. He neither listened to his wife's troubles with their son nor sided with her when Tony publicly derided her; he shied away from conflict as much as he ignored her complaints about his hoarding habits; the only thing that got his attention was his retirement, and that fact wasn't lost on Tony.

With every chance he got, Tony manipulated the situation to pitch his parents against each other. "Mom, your refusal to hire an accountant is not only hurting the company, but also dad's retirement," he once said loud enough so that his father could hear him.

As predicted, Victor marched right over. "What is he talking about? Is that true? Have you not hired a new accountant yet?" He didn't wait for an answer. "How long as it been since we had one?"

She tried to speak, but kept going.

"What are you doing with all my money? I'm out there every day selling, and you don't have an accountant to keep us going? What are you doing all day then?" As he erupted on her Tony took a step back, smiling wickedly.

Back and forth his parents argued until finally Barb stormed off to her office.

"Don't walk away from me! I'm talking to you!"

"Then you can talk to me in my office," she retorted, not wishing to discuss the company's finances so openly or so loudly. Tony yoked his father on.

"I'm worried, dad. I've brought many accounting firms to her, but she keeps turning them down. I'm afraid the company is facing some serious financial issues, and if she's not willing to address them then who is?"

"What kind of issues?"

"Well, for starters, several vendors have already put us on credit hold," he said, playing innocent.

Victor exploded. He barged right into her office and the two began a shouting match that echoed through the building. When he came out he went right to his son.

"You're here more than I am, and I need to know what's going on, and when I retire you're in charge so make sure you know what's going on at all times!"

Tony happily smiled.

Chapter 23

Victor and Barbara

In thirty years of doing business the company had never once held a sales meeting. This was because of a longstanding philosophy of Victor's that sales meetings babysat sales agents, and Victor was not one to hold anyone's hand; if an agent couldn't sell and report his sales then he wasn't worth keeping around, and Victor propagated profit; the higher the better.

Over the years, he had hired an array of sales agents, from mediocre to superb, but he always put the responsibility of recording in the hands of the agent; it was the agent's responsibility- or burden- to track his sales and ensure his commission was accurate, but over the decades those who relied on 100% commissions argued the most with accounting; it became a he-said she-said with many sales agents quitting in anger.

Victor meanwhile wanted as few reports given to him as possible; his idea of a sales meeting was simply to *ask* an agent how the man *felt* he was doing. This left a wide gap for interpretation and an even wider gap in projections; for thirty years, Barb neither knew what sales were coming in, how much money she could expect at the end of the month, or what bills could be paid; it was anybody's guess.

The entire system lacked accountability. And while Tony argued that by purging the sales team he was starting over he didn't install the updated software called accountability 101; he still left that out. He also had no way of improving communication between sales and accounting, and so this remained a contentious point over commissions, which was simply done away altogether and henceforth any future agents, such as Arthur, were paid a fixed salary.

"Know how your product works," Victor told him, encouraging him to put boots on and spend a day with a technician; not wanting to be upstaged Tony also did this, but whereas Arthur worked a long day, Tony complained of a shoulder problem and left at lunch.

Arthur also worked in close proximity with the project management team. Since the majority of decisions went through him this included anything dealing with products, contracts, field measurements, scheduling of technicians, and installs; nothing was done without his prior approval, but his procrastination and evasion only created a traffic jam of queued employees, hoping to grab him before he left again. Not surprisingly, he dashed out of whatever door he could find and the problems piled up.

But despite his evasion sales were booked. In six months, Victor closed over $330,000 in sales at a solid 45% profit margin ($148,500) as well as another $490,000 in service and retrofit sales; Antonio was in charge of service. He further helped out the senior estimator by helping him close nearly $525,000. But selling and technical expertise was the limit of his abilities. He was neither an adept administrator- failing terrifically at organization- nor a manager of others; he bitterly resented managing.

Much like his son, his instructions were often as convoluted and disheveled as his outfit, and to make matters worse he contradicted himself daily, giving Antonio instructions and then shouting at him because he didn't do the opposite; who had time to teach anyone about the Internet when they were too busy changing their mind?

But if Victor's hypocrisy and neglect were not bad enough his hoarding problem exacerbated the situation; the company sacrificed its warehouse and yard for his habit. In the latter he kept disabled vehicles, rusted from years of neglect; one even had become inhabited by raccoons. One insurance agent remarked that the yard resembled a car junkyard more than anything.

Perhaps even more appalling was the warehouse, which is where Victor stored most of his junk; too often his technicians had to work around his hoarding. He stored things in the warehouse that he neither needed nor were relevant to the company's industry, from drums of paint to old bicycles, from a tepee to a generator that was lacking most of its parts, but which he insisted on keeping, because "you never know when it might be needed."

He filled his warehouse with defunct office furniture, broken chairs, locked cabinets with no key, and copiers that were not only obsolete but also broken; he blocked aisles with lawn chairs, and every turn around a corner was placing one's life in danger; there were steel beams he just set loosely on top of crates, and equipment that neither worked properly nor was marked as such and too often was mistaken for something that worked.

And Victor tenaciously defended his habit. "I was born with nothing and I'll die with nothing," he said, "But until then, I'll keep whatever I find." In all this confusion and chaos the technicians were supposed to change in and out of their company supplied uniforms; nobody was allowed to take them home. And ironically, above the doorway in and out of the warehouse was posted a large sign that read, *Safety is everyone's responsibility.*

But Victor was only human. He had as many positives as he had negatives. Where he neglected others and evaded issues he was an expert in his industry, a fact that even his competition recognized and respected. Where he failed to hold others accountable he instead opted for a quasi-policy of laissez-faire, simply setting the example and allowing others to follow. He was hardly a good listener, or for that matter a good communicator, but he made sure his technicians had every tool at their disposal.

He was a man that picked his battles and only the ones he knew he could absolutely win, even when it came to his family. He failed at managing. He failed at listening; he even failed at his marriage, but he still loved his wife and children, no matter how estranged things became; Barb never forgave him for having an affair, but for their children's sake they stay married.

They neither talked with one another in idle discourse nor ate with each other at home; they were as distant as Victor was to clients. Barb denied him intimately, treating him coldly, rejecting both his friendship and advice. She neither sought a divorce nor felt the need to sleep beside him, and so they got a king mattress; distance was very much a part of their marriage.

Like clockwork, she ate without him and then went to bed without him. Meanwhile, he went to the bar, stayed late and slept on the couch; he never once begged for forgiveness or apologized for his affair. Rather instead, he simply moved on. "If you don't like it don't look at it," he reminded her. So, she looked at him as little as possible.

He was a hollow man, void of any emotion it seemed, neglecting both his company and wife, and turning instead to alcohol and hoarding; he evaded her like he did everyone else, withdrawing from the world and not even knowing his son was gay until a year after everyone else found out. Blind to reality, he saw the world through a warped pair of lens, picking his battles, and insisting that his son would inherit the company after him.

Chapter 24

The Glue

"If not for my children," Barb said to Arthur one morning, confiding a deep, dark secret. "I would have divorced Victor." A devout woman, she went to worship every Sunday and believed in the sanctity of family above all else. She had had high hopes for her children, but nowadays she feared for their futures; though she loved Tony she somehow felt that his errors were her fault.

She blamed herself for his homosexuality and took responsibility for his egotism. "I failed as a parent," she said, lowering her head in shame. She loved her children, and she believed she had done her best to raise them. But it apparently her good wasn't good enough.

"Somewhere along the way, I must have done something terribly wrong."

Chapter 25

The Superintendent

When Tony reported no earnings for the month, Barb demanded an answer. He replied unashamedly that he had spent the month starting a business. While she shouted at him for being on the company's dime, Victor applauded his entrepreneurial spirit.

* * * * * * * *

As tenuous as Barb's relationship was with her husband it strained even further when Tony abruptly tried to fire the company's superintendent, Frank. Second only to Victor in technical knowledge, Frank was also the most senior employee. He not only disapproved of Tony's lofty goals and vision for growth, but he voiced them too.

93

In the beginning, he had embraced Tony's ideas as fresh and welcoming, much like everyone else. They were inspiring and innovative, but when they failed to bear fruit he lost faith; overtime, Tony's push for change became less appealing and instead overbearing. He continued to push his cultural overhaul, but after three years and nothing to show for it what good was it? To make matters worse, Tony neither recognized the failure of his ideas nor would have accepted it had he acknowledged it, and thus as he persisted upon it Frank become more vocal in his repudiations.

The final breaking point came when Tony demanded that every employee wear a button or put on a shirt supporting Obama. Frank refused. It wasn't that he was a Republican. It was that Tony was once again pushing his culture to a disillusioned audience like an underperforming magician expecting a standing ovation.

"I'm not wearing this," he said, throwing the button to the floor.

Tony pointed to it. "Yes, you are. You are part of this team and we are all about team spirit here."

"I don't need to wear that button to be a part of this team. Besides, I've been on this team a lot longer than you," he replied harshly. If Tony had realized how much of a failure his ideas had been he would have accepted Frank's argument as reasonable, but such was never the case; the prodigal son refused to allow dissension in the ranks.

"When we support a cause together we move forward together, and we are in a transition of becoming something greater. Now pick up the button and be apart of this new dream team."

But Frank crossed his arms. What a load of crap Tony was. Everyone in the room suddenly flipped back to see what Tony would do; he had fired others for lesser offenses. What would he do now? Would he actually fire Frank over this? It certainly seemed plausible. After all, many that Tony had purged had been non-believers.

Just then though, Barb came storming in and demanded her son stop what he was doing. She was outraged that he would risk jeopardizing the company with a possible blatant lawsuit? The fact that he then alleged she was infringing upon his rights while ignoring the rights of others was simply mind-blowing.

But Tony was undaunted. "I am building a change coalition," he had said, "and that means starting with teamwork, and teamwork is everyone doing what I say."

Frank wasn't the only one to drop his jaw, but even more shocking was that Tony later put it on a company shirt for everyone to wear. Those that refused were fired.

Chapter 26

Frank's Reputation

Tony loved giving orders, but refused to take any. He delegated, but his instructions were often as vague as his lofty ideas. When he fired Amanda in Accounts Receivable, he did so because she failed to read his mind. He alleged it was insubordination and underperformance.

* * * * * * * *

"People should want to grow," he said, spreading his gospel. "This company is about growing and being a part of something greater than just ourselves." He denounced individualism, and yet aspired to be the leader of the company's face-lift. He purged those that defied him, and hired only those that admired him; he hired drug users, alcoholics, thieves, and boasted he had the best technicians in the industry; when they erred one too many times, he publicly fired them in order to elevate his authority.

But for all those that he fired the one he wanted to eliminate the most of all seemed untouchable: Frank had Victor's blessing, and as long as Victor breathed air the man had immunity. After all, Victor and him had history. Long before the company, Victor and he had been technicians, working side-by-side together. When Victor opened up shop he invited Frank to join him; he trusted no other man in the world.

A bulwark of integrity and expertise, Frank was highly regarded by both his co-workers as well as his competition. Clients valued his knowledge, as did his crews; whenever there was a technical issue, technicians sought his advice; especially since Victor wasn't around. Even project managers turned to him whenever schematics didn't match the field conditions.

Despite their obvious differences, Victor and he made a formidable team. While they were both tech savvy Victor was more the salesman, and so while he sold Frank ran the crews; thus, while one trained new sales agents the other trained new technicians. This is what they did for thirty years and it proved to be a complementing relationship, each relying upon the other, putting trust in the other and respecting one another's leadership.

Although Victor was the owner he entrusted Frank with as much authority as he had, making him his unofficial partner in nearly every aspect of the business except finance. Even Barb came to depend upon his expertise, often turning to him when her husband failed to respond. Whenever she couldn't get an answer out of Victor, she simply went to Frank.

Chapter 27

The Company's Crews

Barb valued Arthur as much as she valued Frank, welcoming their conservative perspectives as well as their care and diligence. And perhaps more importantly, they worked quite well together. Neither believed in "rallying the troops" to inspire action; they both shared a contention for lofty ideas, believing instead that modeling the example fostered more productivity than trying to ignite the energy in a room.

They were alike in many ways. Both believed in solid growth, growing the business from the ground up rather than how Tony saw things; they compared notes and shared ideas, talking business only until they were satisfied; Tony could talk for hours. Neither needed the limelight that Tony required, and this did well to improve morale, because Arthur kept a line of communication open that went up and down the ladder; with him, problems became resolved, grievances were heard, and for the first time morale began to elevate; it was this strategic relationship that finally helped to bolster morale.

Frank dedicated himself to his work. He listened to other's ideas, offering his own when needed, and letting his reputation speak for itself. He believed in rewarding based on merit, giving gift cards to his crews as a thank you and earning their respect and loyalty as a result. And since the crews had first pick at the budget they repaid Victor and Frank with high productivity.

Victor promised them forty hours. It was a promise he tried to keep, not always, but he did his best, and it showed. Unlike his son, who put that into writing, Victor was old school, giving his word and shaking on it, a gentleman's agreement; older clients respected it, but younger clients tended to screw over the company.

Nevertheless, Victor never went back on his word. Even if it was a slow week he put his technicians in the shop, billing it to the company as "shop time." This upset Barb, but there was little she could do; the technician was the lifeblood of the company, and Victor and Frank did everything they could to keep that morale up.

And in thirty years, this was a success the two of them shared. Through collaboration and commitment to the crews they brought projects in on time, pleased clients, and earned new business; even those that yelled and screamed for Victor to hurry up always hired him again for their next project; his expertise was second to none. He was the best in the business and even the competition had to admit it; there were projects the competition simply couldn't handle and turned them over to him.

And although they didn't control their market they had a nice slice of the pie. Perhaps more importantly was the preferential treatment they got from clients. No matter the price tag, clients tended to go with him, even new clients were advised by existing clients to go with him. Victor saw things that nobody else did, from minute details to the clear and obvious that seemed to elude all others; he was the defining talent of his industry, sought after by those across the country and even venders called upon him for inquisitive engineering scenarios.

But Frank and Victor did have their moments of disagreement. It was only natural. Sometimes Victor lost. Sometimes Frank did, but no matter what they respected the other's opinion; they both set high standards, pushed their crews, and challenged them with new installs; they imbued each man with a sense of self-accomplishment and congratulated rookies on a job well done. They mentored, offered guidance, and helped technicians learn from mistakes; they were harsh but fair, reprimanding as they rewarded, and always seeking to fill their crews with an immeasurable sense of pride.

"If I can do it, then so can you," Frank often said. "Now I'm gonna push you, and we're all gonna push you, and at times you may hate that, but just bear with us, because we're only doing it to help you." He was optimistic and a strong believer in positive reinforcement.

And time and again, Tony tried to intervene. He had no business asserting any measure of authority, but believed it was the only way to force his father into a position of early retirement; moreover, he wanted Frank gone. The fact that his orders as well as his desire to see the senior foreman dismissed were as counterintuitive as any idea he had thus far.

Chapter 28

Building a Change Coalition

Tony not only tried to interfere in operations, but also tried to undermine Frank and his father. In one case, he fired two technicians in front of Victor, who protested loudly and unmercifully. For 30 minutes, the two laborers were unsure if they were still employed. Eventually, Victor won and the men stayed.

* * * * * * * *

With abysmal sales, morale still low, expensive trips, catalogues collecting dust, and his parents still not talking, Tony once again had a lofty idea. It wasted three months of everyone's time, accomplished nothing, and generated more resentment than revenue.

He entitled his glorious initiative, "Leading Change," and it focused almost entirely on elusive values that few if any could relate to; they were either values the company had never embraced or were so up in the clouds that they didn't catch any footing. One such inspiring phrase was posted on a wall. It read, "When the economy is in winter our company will always be in the spring!"

He hosted – or rather mandated- early morning meetings much like Employee Appreciation Day, only this time there was only coffee. He called these meetings, "adrenaline meetings," and the intent was to get everyone pumped up and excited to go to work; but standing for an hour, being forced to clap and cheer while still waking up was anything but fun. Everyone was required to share his or her weekly goals, give any updates to progress, and keep it short and sweet so that everyone had a turn; Tony went last and took as long as he felt was necessary.

He asked abstract questions like: Why is success a must? What will it give us? How can we be more efficient? What if we are not successful? How will we feel if we do it? He used role-playing and phrases like "Slaying the dragon," which only confused people as to its meaning; at one end it was a good exercise to get everyone to see the big picture, but it ultimately failed to draw interest, because he repeatedly underscored how nobody was working hard enough.

Moreover, he talked about the results of failure more than how success was going to be reached. He had everyone list their fears if the company failed. A few of these included losing one's job, not feeding one's family, not being able to pay the mortgage, less overtime, failing to pay child support, and many more; it was to say the least a very scary list.

But if his intent was to motivate others into action it actually had the opposite effect. Instead, it created panic when all of a sudden his trips and low sales figures were brought to light. All at once the list seemed more realistic than possible. Had he used the opportunity to segue into sales he might have recovered his initiative, but sadly Tony kept right on going, talking about all the things the company could do as opposed to what he could do. He listed so many wonderful things, but what good was a company picnic when there was no money! Overnight his initiative died; all of its momentum was lost. As soon as everyone realized there was no money they dragged their feet.

What good was talking about the future when there was no money now? But Tony kept on going. He talked about fishing trips, being the best in service, expanding into new territories, getting customer feedback, even setting up a "We Care" hotline, but to what end? There was no money; the fact that Barb was borrowing from her retirement was the only reason everyone was still employed. In three months, Tony never spoke a word about revenue strategies, and frankly as the meetings got longer most wondered why he was even there instead of out making sales calls.

He wanted every Monday to feel like a Friday, but this only encouraged people to look forward to the weekend. And while his intentions were noble he failed to express sincerity or gratitude or even acknowledge the sacrifices others had already made; for as much as the ship was sinking many had stayed aboard, believing the company could once again live and breath. But the future was looking even bleaker; his ideas were grandiose and his speech self-centered, his undertone offensive, and too often he dictated the meetings, offering up the same magic trick to a cynical audience.

"We need to feel that sense of accomplishment every day," he said to an unmoved group.

But the cynicism ran deeper. The exposed leaks of his initiative were just the icing; Tony had promised in the

A. Ruben

past, but never delivered. He had offered promotions and bonuses, but cancelled them, explaining that everyone should want to grow. "Everyone should want to make this company a great place to work by going above and beyond what is expected of him or her." Of course, he gave himself a bonus for saving the company money.

He even rewarded himself for his initiative, arguing that he be reimbursed for the business books he purchased to do research; he neither credited the author's nor mentioned the books during his initiative, claiming instead that they were his original ideas. Thus, he wanted to be reimbursed for ideas he claimed were his.

"Each and every one of us is the key to success, and when we are gung-ho as a team we are an unstoppable force!" He ripped that off of a book.

The Numbers

Chapter 29

Accountability

To validate his boast that the company was in fact "international," Tony hired a graphic designer in the Philippines and a marketing specialist in Mexico.

* * * * * * * *

Despite having purged the company's sales force, Tony remained as obstinate as ever that his method was the archetype of growth. "When everyone listens to me and does exactly as I say then we move mountains," he said.

Asserting that he knew best, he further claimed to be the company's top salesman, which was far from accurate. In fact, he was the lowest earning agent at the company, surpassed by his father, his uncle, the senior estimator and even Arthur. Even more shameful, he was further outdone by the company's technicians, who upsold better than he: in one year he sold $680,000, which was exceptional except that he lost most of his profits through negligence, failing to communicate with the project management team and then later denying any accountability for the disasters. In sharp contrast, the senior estimator earned $665,000 that same year at a profit of nearly 20% (about $133,000).

The following year his delinquency continued and despite earning nearly $610,000 he once again netted low margins. From an initial 30% estimated profit, Tony lost half of that through negligence. Nevertheless, he denied responsibility, blamed others, preached his vision, and once more claimed the title of highest salesman. But the facts only shame the boastful:

Together, Victor and Antonio earned just over a million dollars in service and retrofit sales at an average profit margin of 30% (roughly $300,000). Quite pleased with those results, Victor rewarded the crews with gift cards, thanking them for their devotion.

"Sell as high as you can, if you can," he said, taking the time to thank each one personally. Although he preached his philosophy too, his actions had born fruit and so others were inclined to listen. "If you're not selling high, then you're not doing your job right." He was generous in his appreciation as he was tyrannical about his standards.

He didn't waste money. Unlike his competition that entertained clients, Victor sold on his reputation. He believed winning clients wasn't through expensive dinners or outings to football games, but with expertise. He had a sense of humor and he used it too. "Know what you're talking about and make them laugh, and I promise you they'll remember you." And it was that advice that made Arthur the number one salesman at the company.

In the same year that Tony earned $610,000, Arthur booked over $1,200,000 at an average profit margin of 35% (about $420,000). But he wasn't done yet. In addition to that, he also secured the largest contract the company had ever had, $5,000,000. At 28% margin, he earned the company $1,400,000. Thus, of a grand total of $6,200,000, he earned just over $1,800,000 profit.

Chapter 30

Obliviousness

Tony dismissed his poor sales figures by reiterating his role as the company's visionary. "You're looking at a CEO," he told Arthur. "My job isn't to generate sales, but to inspire others to do that for me."

* * * * * * * *

Having promoted himself to sales manager, he neither had any interest in accepting the responsibility nor had any interest in becoming an effective one. "When you're born to lead, it just comes naturally." He started holding sales meetings; somehow believing this was clear proof of his natural leadership he neither reviewed figures nor discussed strategy at any of the meetings.

Instead, he used the time to propagate his ideas, holding the team "hostage" for hours on end as he relished the sound of his own voice. In one case, a meeting lasted for an unbelievable six hours.

"I have so many ideas," he said excitedly. "I just need people to listen, and execute on them." He could hardly sit still as he talked about culture, vision and growth, which he emphasized over and over again as if everyone had missed it the first time around. He didn't necessarily expand on them as much as he simply reiterated himself, recanting on their importance over everything else.

He boasted that being a CEO was in his blood, alleging that, "some people are just born to be leaders." And yet, he failed to hold himself accountable on more than one occasion. He neglected customers and sales, going so far as to offend one, which just so happened to be the company's oldest and most profitable client: in a shocking move he pulled out of the negotiations that were moving strongly in the company's favor and instead issued an ultimatum- it was not only an insult to the client but highly unfavorable to the company.

Not surprisingly, the client decided the time had come to part ways; it took Victor and Arthur several months to bring the client back, and even then the client was reluctant. Why then did Tony think it was a brilliant idea to insult the client again? And this time he did it to the man's face. Nobody knew why, but Tony only smiled. "I just saved the company from a clogged artery of bad cholesterol," he said.

Chapter 31

Pulling Hair

"My job ends at the handshake," Tony declared, dictating where the boundaries of his responsibilities ended. "I don't do anything with operations."

Subsequently, this left the project management team to guess on most of the details of his sale. When and if he did interact with them, Tony did nothing but preach or interfere with other's sales: in one instance, Arthur booked a $450,000 deal at 20% margin (about $90,000). It wasn't great, but he had been working on the deal for over a year and was expected to get it. Instead of applauding his hard work, Tony inexplicably called up the supplier and rejected the manufacturer's generous discount. Suddenly, Arthur stood to make significantly less profit. Tony then accused him of pursing unprofitable projects.

A few days later, he booked his own $450,000 deal, demanding praise for it and paraded around the office gloating about how he was going to make 1% profit margin on it, or just $4,500.

Chapter 32

Reports and Tracking

With the company straddling on bankruptcy, Barb had no choice but to pull from her own bank account. She refused to let her company die, and so instead of planning for her retirement, she began drawing from it to stay afloat.

* * * * * * * *

Having graduated with a degree in marketing, Tony advertised his vision nonstop. "I am about leading change," he said, inviting others into his circle that shared in his beliefs as well as enthusiasm. He was passionate about his ideas and extremely charismatic when it came to expressing them to new people.

"The key to achieving in life is to be surrounded by people who are already successful," he once told Arthur.

And yet, he had fired an intern who showed promise, redefining success according to his reality. "It's not about jumping higher," he had told the intern. "It's about jumping higher when I say so."

He believed in hiring slow, but firing fast; he failed to train, kept unrealistic deadlines and standards, and purged with delight. "People need to rise to the occasion," he told Arthur. "That's why it's so important for others to observe someone who is as successful as myself. That's why I'm a lighthouse for others. I guide them to their own success. I help people take control of their lives, and reach their goals; what limits a person is only his or her own internal stopping sign." And yet in three years, he dismissed nine interns and purged sixty employees.

Perhaps even more amazing is how often Tony demanded everyone applaud him for the purges. "We are leading the change!"

Chapter 33

The Critical Number

In addition to purging the sales team, Tony also inexplicably scrapped the sales tracking and recording practices, replacing it with telekinesis. Henceforth, he wanted everyone to read his mind, insisting that failure to read it was no excuse. "Only when we think alike can we grow together."

Barb took up the crusade again and asked Arthur to institute a new tracking process. "I need answers and I need you to help us get back on track." She was completely in the dark and with bills stacking up she needed help right away; if it wasn't obvious to anyone it was certainly to her. This was part of Tony's plan of taking control of her department: he would blacken everything, hold back as much as he could and then accuse her of sabotaging the company in order to relieve her of her duties. It might have worked had she not had the services of Arthur.

Right away, he proposed a three-fold plan. First, Arthur proposed creating new tracking spreadsheets, which he also suggested adding a universal critical number in order to help guide every sales endeavor. She asked what he meant by that. He explained it for her. A critical number was an accountability marker to ensure profitability as well as maintaining consistent projections.

"So it's a profit percentage?"

"Not quite." Designed to filter sales leads the critical number was a date on the calendar more than anything else. Arthur set it at 90 days. So, if he followed up on a lead he had to know if the client was serious, and by asking point-blank if the client was prepared to sign within 90 days he filtered out his leads.

While the company did filter its method was poor to say the least: as long as it was related to the industry the company pursued it; Arthur narrowed that. He meant to be far more stringent. He wanted to know specifics and if the client wasn't willing to give him a definite answer then he moved on; it was all about who was serious and who was a waste of time, and time was money.

Moreover, ninety days was a business quarter. By knowing what sales were expected ninety days out the accounting team could forecast ahead; bills could now be paid far in advance, fleet maintenance could be regularly scheduled, and contingencies could be planned; more money meant more options, and it all came down to that critical number; nothing else mattered but that.

The idea of a critical number wasn't radical, or even his invention. Hardly. He had read about it in literature as a mainstream device, and immediately saw its advantages. The question remained could it work? Well, Arthur had been doing it himself, but could it apply to the whole team; would others be receptive to it? Barb wasn't sure. She liked the idea a lot, but was concerned about the loss of leads. Arthur's critical number would mean slashing leads by over half. Could the company risk that?

"We already filter," he said, assuaging her worries. "But we spend more time chasing leads than we do racing after good ones. If we put our time into those good leads then we haven't really lost anything."

"So you want us to turn away business?"

"Yes," he agreed. "Because there's good leads and there's great leads."

"But how does that increase our chances of getting more work? Just because you filter, doesn't mean your chances have improved."

He shook his head. Not true at all.

Just then the phone rang. It was a prospective client. "Here, let me demonstrate," he said, taking the call. As she watched, Arthur ran the client through a series of short questions that were direct and straight to the point. He probed for information, identifying first and foremost if the client was shopping around. That was his first red flag.

His questions identified specific information that Barb was surprised any client would give. He learned what product the customer was interested in, narrowed down a date for discussing a quote, and getting a decision for signing; never in a million years did Barb ever think she could get such valuable information in so short a phone call. When Arthur finished he had the client's name, his number, and a timetable for the next action. She was beside herself with amazement.

"Make it happen," she said in wonderment.

Chapter 34

Ninety Days

Unlike Tony's strong-arm approach, Arthur was tactful, advising through suggestions. He supported Barb's ideas, adding to them, and presenting any opinions that her employees had. In sharp contrast to her son's overbearing pompous attitude and sense of self-importance was not only demeaning but also was counterproductive, Arthur welcomed ideas. He didn't dismiss any new ideas, but rather instead opened the floor up for discussion; he looked at notes and historic patterns such as trade shows to judge whether they were worth the cost.

He opened his door to others and at once ideas poured in. Everyone had an opinion to improve the company; when Tony claimed the deluge of ideas came from his inspiring leadership Arthur just ignored him. He had too much work to do.

Chapter 35

Forecasting Ahead

"Our job is to book sales," Arthur said to Barb, respectfully. "Let us worry about the sales. You just plan ahead for us." She smiled back at him, pleased at his efforts.

* * * * * * * *

Right away, his sales strategy was received positively. He took charge of the sales meetings, using an agenda and substantially reduced the time down to less than twenty minutes; sales meetings were to be quick and to the point. He modeled his client questions to the team, and by the end of the month the results were already showing. The company was filtering more stringently, booking deals with higher margins, and achieving fewer problems on jobsites.

A. Ruben

From sales to estimating, service to upselling, the company was turning away millions of dollars in favor of ideal business; while it was contemporary it was nonetheless a risky move, but Barb trusted Arthur and her trust paid off. By the end of the first quarter, morale had skyrocketed and profit margins had never been higher; accounting's projections started paying bills in advance, which not only eased venders but also rebuilt confidence. All at once, the company was given extended credit lines; the critical number had brought about a golden age.

"I'm making you the sales manager," said Barb one day. Arthur didn't know what to say but thank you. Then he remembered Tony was the sales manager.

"I'm making you the official one," she said. My son gave himself that title, but you earned it."

Chapter 36

Colliding Ideals

Barb never needed to demote Tony. His self-promotion had never been official. Thus, promoting Arthur to sales manager was easy.

* * * * * * * *

After thirty years in business, Barb was now faced with the most difficult decision of her career, either lose her retirement and save her company, or allow her son to bankrupt the company. Since he came aboard four years earlier he had accomplished nothing except creating higher turnover, plunging morale, escalated costs, and stripped the company of loyal clients.

She put all the blame on him. Although she loved him he simply had no concept of how to run a business. He

127

was self-centered, egotistical, manipulative, cold-hearted and uncaring. He pretended to love, but it was never sincere; he spun reality to fit his needs, demanding from others but never reciprocating. He pushed his agenda upon others, and rejected any ideas except his own.

In sharp contrast, Arthur was elastic, capable, receptive to new ideas, supportive and accountable; he showed his love to Sallie as well as to the company and for that Barb included him in the succession plan. It was a great honor to bestow upon him, but unfortunately only served to fuel Tony's bitter resentment. Every day he clashed with Arthur, disagreeing with his every decision and making his every effort near impossible; they were polar opposites, from culture and growth to supervision and vision; whereas Arthur was calculated and approached growth with pace, Tony tried to spark it through zeal, energizing others to rally around an evangelical spirit of excitement.

Chapter 37

Booking Projects

After six months of success, Arthur had killed two birds with one stone. Morale was restored and so were the company's finances.

* * * * * * * *

While clashing with Arthur, Tony took all the credit for the company's success. To prove how brilliant he was as a natural born leader he began giving away contracts for free. One such project was worth $56,000. Another was for $64,000. Barb was furious, but he just dismissed her complaints as silly, alleging that the company could always write it off as a tax credit either to charity or a loss.

"Part of growing a company is building public awareness to our name. You have to give to receive." He

129

then donated another project worth $84,000. Each one of his giveaways put a strain on the company's resources, including time and manpower; he insisted that technicians work on his free projects before working on profitable ones. The fact that he lost an additional $18,000 because of his negligence only infuriated Barb more.

With a grand total of over $200,000 in free giveaways the company took an even bigger hit with Tony's sales. Of a $120,000 deal he made less than $10,000 in profit. In a $174,000 contract he went negative. In a final $140,000 deal, he lost half of his margin after exasperating the project management team with his aloofness, neglect, and lack of response to their questions; despite the success of everyone else it meant that the rest of the company had to offset Tony's losses and thus not grow.

For instance, in that same time, Arthur booked a deal at $135,000 at 74% profit margin ($99,900). Another at $62,000, netting 81% profit, or just over fifty thousand dollars, and then a third contract at $56,000 with a margin of 73%, or almost $41,000. So, regardless of how well he did the company strained because of Tony.

"We are about creating a name for ourselves," the visionary son said, defending his giveaways. "Being a business is more than just numbers. It's about being a part of the community, giving back, and taking that bold first step in leading change forward."

Chapter 38

Project Management

Barb had had it. Even if Arthur succeeded, her son was killing the company. "I need your help, and so will my daughter when the two of you marry. Without you, this company is doomed."

* * * * * * * *

For thirty years, Victor expected his sales team to collaborate with the project management team. By doing so, everyone could resolve problems before they exacerbated, and yet Tony refused to cooperate, viewing such teamwork as both ludicrous and beneath him. After his last purge the only agents left at the company- if they could be called that- were Victor, Tony, Antonio, the senior estimator, and Arthur, the core skeleton of the company.

But while Arthur was the sales manager and was the driving force behind its recent success Tony continued to believe he was; Barb neither corrected this fact nor wished Arthur to alter it. She asked him to keep silent. And so, as the silent sales manager, reporting exclusively to her and driving the company behind the scenes he had to endure the agony of Tony taking all the credit as well as taking it a step further and insisting that all sales, regardless of their nature, filter through him first. Tony not only wanted to control the sales leads but also filter them in lieu of how Arthur had modeled.

"As the sales manager, I am responsible for any and all sales of this company, no matter in what capacity."

He then asserted that his father and uncle report to him, which his father only laughed at and walked out the door; it wasn't that easy for Antonio, whose desk sat nearby. In no time at all, Antonio was doing his nephew's bidding as well as trying to follow his brother's directions, and when they contradicted he received the brunt of both of their displeasure.

"When we are committed we achieve amazing results," said Tony, spreading his evangelistic ideas; for whatever reason, he expected everyone to eagerly come in on the weekend and work without pay. "Growth happens when everyone is aligned on the same page." And yet, his vision lacked as much coherency as it did sensibility.

He pushed others to sell including technicians, but his giveaways did nothing to endear him to the technicians who couldn't upsell on a free contract; the client thought that any upsells would be free too. And while they were paid by the hour they took pride in their ability to upsell, to get referrals, and to be a part of Arthur's reforms; they knew he was the mastermind behind it and gave him every respect they could.

They applauded Arthur, but never in the presence of Tony. They shook his hand and congratulated him on achieving what they always believed was possible; they were loyal to the company and the tenure among them averaged 14 years; for the longest time they wanted to see growth, but not the kind Tony published.

They resented his dictatorial orders, his tyrannical approach to leadership, his vague instructions, and his hypocrisy in holding others accountable but never himself; the fact that he expected others to read his mind was simply ridiculous. And frankly, they detested working on projects that didn't make any money; they took pride in their work but cared about the company. What good was working on a project that didn't even pay the bills; what future was there in projects like that?

Even when Tony erred and had them work overtime or even double time they resented him, because he never made it easy. He always overworked them, always. In one instance he gave away an $86,000 project and then re-scheduled all the labor for the weekend. So instead of having any break in their exhausting week they were now expected to work Saturday and Sunday to the point of breaking and be ready to go Monday morning bright and early. They weren't slaves, but they certainly felt like it.

Even the project management team sympathized with the crews. When Tony sold a $92,000 deal it seemed like he was getting back on track, but only then did they realize he had sold discontinued products. All at once, this meant an increase in costs to persuade the factory to put it back on the assembly line to manufacture; for the loss it took he might as well have given it away.

In yet another embarrassment, he matched a competitor's price and then paraded around the office having others stop what they were doing to applaud him. When it was discovered he had failed to measure and that his competitor had bid the wrong product he was stuck with the contract as well as almost $10,000 in additional costs to give the client what he really needed.

In a final disgrace, Tony bid a two-phase project. He was awarded the first phase, but had put no profit into it, assuring the company that he had the second phase in the bag. Of course, when a competitor suddenly undercut his price he tried unsuccessfully to match it and lost the second phase. Now he had no profit and a stack full of problems from the first phase. "It is what it is," he said, wiping his hands clean and going after his next sale. "I am a visionary, not operations."

Chapter 39

Further Suggestions

If his giveaways and negligent sales weren't bad enough, he further disgruntled his clients. When they called the office to complain he handed the phone over to his mother. "It's your company. You need to be hearing what customers are saying." When she tried to put the blame back on him he simply dismissed it, stating that it was the fault of others.

"Being a visionary is hard work," he said, feeling the need to take another vacation. "It's a marvelous feeling to know that others are supporting your efforts." Whatever delusionary world he was living in came at a heavy cost for the company that desperately tried to pick up after him like a kid leaving his toys everywhere.

Whenever there was a problem he pointed the finger. Whenever there was success he claimed it. He had no shame publicly disrespecting the technicians or staff or even his family. He verbally abused them in front of others, ridiculing them and blaming them for failures of his own; this sharply contrasted with Arthur, who had others bend over backwards to help him; the fact that Arthur greeted them instead of them being obliged to greet him like Tony insisted went miles.

He valued feedback, organized the warehouse, and expanded his strategy to bring cohesion into the company; he listened to other's grievances and resolved matters quickly; he sold as he supervised, empowering others and bringing out the best in their qualities; he sold at higher margins, giving the company more options, and allowing for the purchases of new tools for the crews. He did all this without every asking for a thank you; if this was to be Arthur's company one day he wanted it to run efficiently and productively while at its peak morale.

He earned Frank's respect, which went a long way in getting his projects done before Tony's; crews had to draw straws just because they didn't want to work on Tony's projects. Under Arthur, the warehouse was not only organized but also gained a spacious workspace as well as a better changing area for the technicians. It took a few months, but when it was done Victor congratulated him; if his crews were happy then so was he.

After that, Arthur organized the lot, cleaning away debris, recycling any unused steel and aluminum; he had broken vehicles towed away as well as equipment, and any cash went to Victor, and even had several warehouse doors repaired; the company had only ever used half, limiting its productivity. But Arthur wasn't done yet.

To assist Antonio, he had installed six large marker boards to schedule technicians, one board per day; the weekend went on a single board. Before this, Antonio had been using one board to cover an entire week. Now Antonio could write clearly and didn't need to struggle to fit an entire week on one board. He thanked Arthur and asked him to give him another six so that he could plan two weeks in advance. Suddenly, the Service Department was able to forecast ahead just like accounting.

From chaos to an efficient, highly organized, well-oiled machine, Arthur had transformed the company. He had done the impossible, and the results showed; Barb couldn't be more proud of him. He had compromised with Victor's hoarding, improved morale, enhanced sales, and given the company a new lease on life. He still clashed with Tony, but it was expected.

Almost everyone was pleased with him. Frank shook his hand, hailing him as a worthy future leader of the company, praising his potential. "You didn't have to do any of this, but you did because you wanted to. I respect that."

It was a great time for Arthur, but Tony bitterly resented his limelight being stolen. To punish the crews he introduced an emergency service program; he neither discussed it with his father or Frank. Right away, he laid down the rules. He expected each technician to be ready at a second's notice, even after a long day; there would be no rotation. Tony wanted it random. Moreover, he wanted each technician to be on-call during the weekend, but that meant having to sit by the phone all weekend long.

Frank objected. Unless the company was willing to pay a technician to sit by the phone then there needed to be a rotation. Otherwise a man couldn't spend time with his family. But Tony disagreed. A technician could certainly be with his family. He just had to be ready to leave at any second. The debate went back and forth.

"Don't get me wrong," said Frank. "I think such a program is a good idea, but maybe working out the details first is important before we just right into it."

Tony again refused. It wasn't his problem to sort out the details. He was simply the visionary.

"Then let's talk about overtime," replied Frank, getting impatient at his arrogance. "Saturday and Sunday are overtime. Is the company going to pay for that?"

"Why should the company be expected to pay for something that is already part of the job?"

"Working forty hours is the job. Anything extra is extra. That's how it is."

Tony shook his head. "Absolutely not. If I am a visionary twenty-four hours a day, seven days a week then a technician at this company needs to think that way. How can we move forward when someone only thinks part-time?"

Chapter 40

Arrogance and Disrespect

In addition to expecting others to work out the
details he remained stubborn about not paying for anyone
to sit by the phone. "People should want to grow," he said,
"Your job is to help this company grow."

But no matter how hard Frank opposed him it
seemed that nothing could penetrate that thick skull. "We
are all loyal to this company, and we want it to grow, but
not for free; we have to eat. If you want these men to work
on the weekends then they need to be paid for their time."

"Absolutely not. Part of their job description is to
be available at all hours."

"For pay, yes, but not for free."

He shook his head. "No, no, no, absolutely not. I
come in on the weekends without asking to be paid,
because that's how I give back to this company."

"That's your choice, but I'm putting my foot down and telling you that they will be paid for their time."

"That's not in the contract."

"You want to challenge the union?" He was all too ready to do it. If Tony was going to press it then he would invite him to the table; against the union, Tony was doomed to fail.

"Of all people I would expect you to guide our future," he replied, shaming him. "We're taking steps to help us move forward and what we need right now are leaders not obstacles."

"I do what my contract says."

"Then perhaps it's time to reconsider your leadership at this company."

"Are you firing me?"

"You are an employee of this company, and like anyone else you are replaceable."

"You didn't answer my question."

But Tony wouldn't answer him. "This company is growing, and right now your actions are going against that direction. Now, we are a team and that means going above and beyond what is asked. I need you to want to be a part of something greater than yourself, because that's what makes a team great. I need you to stop wasting precious time and start agreeing with what I say, so we can grow to the next level."

"I go with what my contract says."

"I'm sorry you feel that way."

Chapter 41

Visionary Drive

Tony hired a new technician named Troy, who happened to be an old friend of his. The intent was to replace Frank with more agreeable blood.

* * * * * * * *

Tony took swift action to ensure his vision was embraced. "Leading change requires a push," he said, enrolling his sister at the local university without her consent; he insisted it was for her own good. Then he did the same to his own mother. "Education is the basis of success." She replied by threatening to fire him. When he ignored her she threatened to take the tuition out of his paycheck; his answer was to publicly shame her.

In a humiliating display before the entire company he denounced her as incompetent; referring to the last fifteen years of fiscal reports he cornered her. "The only way we can grow as a company is by growing ourselves." He alleged he was only doing what was best for her and the company; she pointed her finger at him in disgust. Who was he to speak like that to her? She had been running the business for over thirty years; she had no need for a pompous little brat telling her how to run things.

"I'm just trying to help," Tony said, vindicating his actions. "I educate myself. I meet with other successful business leaders to learn what they do, and I take every opportunity to become a more successful leader. That's what leaders who care do, but I haven't seen you do that. What I do see is you coming in and leaving everyday without every once talking with other employees; nobody knows you exist. You're like a ghost. I just want to help my mother be the best owner she can be. That's why I travel to meet different leaders and learn from them."

"If you want to help then you can start by paying me back for every mistake you've made here, starting with all of your trips!"

He shook his head. She just didn't get it. "I don't think you understand what I've done here. I've cut costs. I cut away the fat that was robbing this place. You and dad had salespeople that sapped this place dry; they did as they pleased, coming and going without any accountability. They reported to nobody and you had no idea if they sold anything or not.

"Now we have excellent sales reporting, weekly sales meetings and flash reports to give us quick insight into how the company is doing; our numbers are updated and you and Sallie know what's going on each and every day. I've done all of this, because I want this company to grow. I want you to reach that dream you've always had of this company growing to the next step.

"I've done so much for this company and yes I've made tough decisions. I've had to fire people, but that's only because I have to do what you and dad refuse to do; you hired mediocrity and when you do that you can't expect to get impressive results. When you hire mediocrity that's what you get. But if you feel the need to blame me then go right ahead, but I've only done what I believed was in the best interest of this company. If anything you should be giving me a bonus." She couldn't help but laugh.

Meanwhile, Victor did his best to stay out of it; family or not he kept his distance. That was until Tony abruptly signed him up for a gym membership and charged it to the company; with a personal trainer the initial bill came to $3,000. "Growing the business begins with growing our minds and bodies."

He then volunteered Arthur's time to a local boy scout troop, promising them everything under the sun; he paraded Arthur's network connections and loyalty like precious gems in tribute, promising them a world traveler, an expert organizer, new equipment paid for by Arthur, and unrivaled adventures; he filled their heads with pipedreams, swept them up in enthusiasm, and gave assurances that Arthur had all the time in the world to guide their young minds.

He had them at world travels, but the only trip they got was disappointment. Arthur could not possibly spare a second. Although he was an Eagle Scout and valued the scouting program there was no way he could devote his time away from the company; although he wished to give back to scouting he did so by trying to use the principals of scouting to build a company, hire new employees, and turn a dream into reality.

But his argument fell on deaf ears. Tony only shamed him for letting the troop down. "Those young men were looking to you. If you can't lead them then maybe you can't lead this company." If it wasn't clear before it was crystal clear now. Tony was trying to sabotage him.

Chapter 42

Getting Everything

Sallie resented her brother for enrolling her. "If I wanted to do it then I would do it," she retorted angrily. "I don't need you running my life!" Yet, she nevertheless gave in and took the courses.

* * * * * * * *

Right away, Tony usurped Frank's authority by assigning his new hire, Troy, as one of the crew leaders. This was met with immediate protest, because a crew leader was meant to be an experienced technician, and Troy was not. Thus, what exactly qualified him to be a crew leader? But Tony would not listen. "It is what it is," he said.

Although Frank was irritated he quickly realized the real victim here was Troy; if anyone had an awkward position it was he. With an unfair bulls-eye on him, Troy neither wanted to be crew leader nor incur the wrath of his fellow technicians; all he really wanted to do was learn the ropes, earn respect, and work his way up to crew leader; he might have been Tony's friend, but humility was a far more enduring quality of his.

Frank recognized this and offered to mentor him; although he didn't like the idea of him as a crew leader he wasn't about to sacrifice quality and workmanship for something as trivial as Tony's decision; the only one not flexible at the company was Tony. And so, pulling him aside, he began to teach him.

Troy happily accepted the offer. Like an foreigner in a strange land, he did not ask for the welcome he got, and was seriously considering quitting just to escape the narrow glares sniping him; he may have been Tony's friend, but right now he didn't care for him very much. "I can't thank you enough," he said, expressing his modesty. If the superintendent was willing to accept him than perhaps others might as well. And in fact once he had the entire affair died down.

Unfortunately, Tony utterly and completely misperceived this as a marvel to his leadership; just has he asked in interviews what the greatest misperception others had of that individual his was believing in the fact that he knew what he was doing. How else could this be explained except for his genius? He had been pushy, but it paid off. Surely that was evidence of his brilliance? Never mind the fact that the wheels had to keep spinning and Frank recognized that. Thus, as Tony paraded around the office expecting handshakes from everyone, he proved yet once again how much of an embarrassment he was

But a faux pas is excusable if one learns from one's mistakes. Tony didn't. He took his apparent success a step further and went to the union hall. There he insisted that the technicians not be paid to sit by the phone; they laughed in his face, protested spiritedly, yielded ground, began to plead, and then disgracefully capitulated. He simply would not take no for an answer, and like a spoiled child he stubbornly held onto his argument: employees were his sole property to do as he pleased; if a person wished to leave he or she was fully entitled to do so, but as long as they were employed by the company they worked day and night for his benefit.

"This is a joke right," asked the representative. "Why would I ever agree to this?"

"Because you want something and so do I."

"And what exactly is it that I want?"

"Membership," Tony said, holding all cards. "The unions aren't doing well. Membership is down, and so what you need is what I can give you. All I need is a yes."

The fact that the hall agreed stunned the crews, Frank as well as Victor; this went beyond betrayal. It was a huge stab in the back for an organization that the workers thought had their best interests in mind, but as it turned out had only its interests in mind. In exchange for agreeing to the present the hall got a promise for the future; they were desperate for membership and Tony played right to that.

In grand celebration of this colossal feat he held a companywide meeting that required every technician to shake his hand in gratitude. It was the single most awkward moment in the company's history, but Tony only gleamed with radiance, his head filled with delusionary images of everyone congratulating him; and to return the favor for their loyalty, he announced, there would be a change in labor hours.

Suddenly, he had their attention. How so? They exchanged looks of curiosity. What exactly did he mean? Did he mean a reduction or increase? It was the latter; he happily announced that in lieu of an 8-hour day each and every technician would now have a 12-hour day along with an emergency service call afterwards; the only one excited was Tony. He was simply beside himself with joy!

Chapter 43

Leverage

Barb cursed the day her son was ever born. Was he trying to kill the life of the company? Unashamedly, he replied, "I'm just a concerned future CEO looking out for his inheritance."

* * * * * * * *

But his string of victories in his father's arena was only just the beginning. After bullying his mother she too gave in to hiring a new accounting firm. It wasn't that she didn't want to hire one. It was that she didn't want to hire one of his picks; she saw right through his persistence: he was still scheming to infiltrate her department and somehow gain control of it; he gave her a grateful hug that was not reciprocated.

155

"Now we're moving in the right direction," he said happily. "At last, we can work more closely together."

But as the saying goes, give them an inch and they take a mile, and that was no truer than with Tony. Now that she had yielded to an accounting firm he pushed for her to agree to his coaching firm.

"In order to grow we need to see where we want to grow and a coach will help us with that."

"Why do I need a coach? I've been running this company for thirty years. I know what I'm doing. I don't need to keep spending all this money when I have none!"

"You and dad did a good job bringing the company to this point, but to get beyond three million dollars you have to do things differently. That's what a coach will do. That's what any good team has, a coach."

"Have you seen how much he is? It's insane!"

"If you want to grow you have to hire the best."

She refused until she could no longer do so; he badgered her daily, pestering her until he even began calling her at night or coming over to the house, shaming her during a family dinner for being so irresponsible with the lives of so many employees; he harassed her until she finally had had enough and gave in.

The new coach's name was Tom, and although Barb had resented hiring him his first impression was certainly lasting. He was neither welcoming to Tony's vision of how to grow the company nor naïve to his enthusiasm and passion; he was experienced, blunt, and sharp with his criticism. He welcomed ideas, but had no qualm about tossing them off the table; the focus was and would remain on the group's success, not an individual's.

His mantra was that cash was king and cliental spoke highly to that. Of his clients many included Fortune 500 companies, and that fact wasn't lost on anyone like Tony, who desperately wanted to get his hands on those business channels. But Tom understood leverage and kept his client list just but far enough away to salivate the selfish and ambitious.

He invited Tony to share his vision, but treated it no differently than anyone else's ideas, which stung like poison to him; more than once, Tony tried to ascend his ideas, but Tom kicked them right off the mountain; no amount of charisma, enthusiasm, or ego under the guise of passion could persuade Tom. Instead, he simply thanked Tony for sharing, offering nothing more than a token smile.

This wasn't what Tony expected when he selected him and as politely as he could without risking the Fortune

500 connections he tried to remind Tom of his place. The coach simply thanked him for offering his opinion, but kindly reminded him that Barb was his client, not him.

At their first meeting with Tom, the entire family was present including Arthur. Tony protested this, but Tom again cordially reminded him that Barb was the client and could pick and choose who she wished to attend her meetings; this included excluding anyone too. Tony shut his mouth. "What I'd like to do first is meet with each and every one of you individually," he said to them. "Ideally, this meeting will be private, and I'll start with Barb."

"That sounds wonderful," said Tony volunteering to join them. "I'll come along."

But Tom stopped him. "I'm first meeting with the owners and then the rest of the executive team."

"Of course," he said, not understanding. "As a future owner I have stock in any conversation about this company. So, lead the way."

Tom could already see Tony would be a problem, but then this wasn't his first rodeo; he had experience with such individuals, and knew exactly how to check their egos.

"Are you an owner right now?"

"I am, yes."

"But you just said you're going to be one later."

"Right now I'm the visionary of this company," he said, evading the question. "The culture of this company is such that it's just as important to be an owner as it is to be the visionary, and up to this point the success of this company has been largely due to me."

"Then I look forward to hearing about that when we speak privately. But right now you're not an owner."

Tony tried again. "As a future owner, it's important for me to be involved in every step of our company's growth. If I'm not there then what message does that say about our ability to be transparent?"

"But again, you're not an owner at this moment, and that's who I'm meeting with." He didn't insult Tony, or even refute his titles. He simply remained professional and stayed on point, refusing to be distracted by anything else; Tony could shine like the rainbow, but Tom was only black and white.

If not for the lure and appeal of the client list Tony would certainly have pressed his luck; his pride was hurt and his ego pained with the indignity of being ignored. All he wanted to do was fire Tom, but the prospect of getting to those contacts was too great to let go. But the worst part about it was that Tony suspected that the coach knew that; the fact that someone else held all the strings was intolerable.

And in fact Tom did. Over the years, he had met many reckless idealists, and while the money was good he felt defeated when ego crucified a company; what good was his advice if it didn't lead to sustaining growth? The fact was that Tony was just another in a long line of grandiose, larger-than-life leaders, who painted a compelling picture of life and called it art; actively self-promoting, completely unsympathetic even to the woes of family, his narcissism demanded the front page of magazines and headline news.

It wasn't to say Tony didn't have qualities, or that his personality was inherently flawed, but narcissism has its reaches. While a charismatic orator that rallied the crowd his rage was trigger happy; anything that didn't feed his grandiosity or personal ideologies was dismissed, which included anything on the scale from hesitation to outright obstruction. He basked in the limelight, but at the expense of others, and in this case jeopardizing his parent's company as well as the livelihood of those employees.

But Tony was not just about leaving a legacy, but being the engine behind the world's legacy. He believed he was as gifted as he was productive; the fact that he had never worked a single day earning minimum wage was to him a sign that he was destined for greatness; as though he were on a mountaintop looking down he treated others inferior, even family. But whereas others saw this and grinded their teeth he felt accomplished; he saw no reason why he shouldn't ask for a handshake from a technician that he overworked. How was coddling going to sharpen that employee into reaching his maximum potential?

What did it matter how he treated others, so long as they worked harder for his benefit; if he had to inspire others by parading around the office then so be it; the fact that he recognized their very existence should be a blessing. And if he didn't practice what he preached it's only because his vision required mobility.

<u>Chapter 44</u>

The Greatest Threat

Under the new 12-hour work schedule the crews experienced a higher rate of fatigue and error, but Tony only viewed that as underperformance. During the hot days of summer he laughed when they asked him for some cold water. In winter, he made them drive in blizzard snow.

* * * * * * * *

Tom began by asking four questions. First, what did he/she feel were the three strengths of the company? Next, what were the three weaknesses, or limitations, of the company? Third, what opportunities existed for growth? And finally, were there any threats that he/she felt might impede growth? Barb began by speaking about her son.

"I see," he said, listening carefully as she elaborated on Tony's purges, his negligent management, his liberal use of vacation time, his idealism and unrealistic expectations as well as his excessive expenditures. She also noted how they repeatedly argued, especially over his leases and furniture for future branch offices. "I never gave my approval for that," she added, noting his strong-armed approach in forcing her to make decisions, including hiring an accounting firm as well as Tom; he took no offense.

"My cash flow is strapped," she said exasperated. "Now I'm forced to take from my personal savings just to keep this company afloat!" And to add insult to injury, she pointed out that she ever since her son came aboard she hadn't been able to collect rent from the company; the building and company were separate entities. In this way, Barb could actually cut herself a check for rent; it was a typical business practice. And rent was just $5,000 monthly.

But ever since Tony had started working at the company sales had plummeted and she had been forced to forgo collecting any rent, which amounted to $60,000 a year for a period of five years. That was $300,000! And the fact that she was draining from her retirement only painted a far direr portrait of the situation.

"I can't stand him," she said, venting her frustration. "And all he wants me to do is retire nowadays."

"Do you want to?"

She chuckled unhappily. "Like I can."

He nodded. "So who runs this company?"

"What do you mean? I do."

He shook his head. "From what you're saying, it doesn't sound like that. Instead what I'm hearing is an undisciplined pursuit of lofty goals running the show." He was blunt. "This isn't about you, or your husband, or even your family. This is about your business, and right now you need to take charge, because from what I'm hearing that isn't happening. Now who controls the finances?"

"I do." That was good to hear. The instant an idealistic heir child gained control of the finances the game was pretty much over; he had many clients in the past that lost out to their narcissist children.

"Alright," he said, helping her. "Let's remember that cash is like oxygen. We need it or we die. So whoever controls the cash also controls the company. I need you to remember that, because things are about to get more difficult before they get easy."

Chapter 45

Ignorance is Bliss

Tom interviewed Sallie next. From his experience it was always good to hear from siblings, especially those who didn't share the same grandiose qualities; typically what he had found was increased tensions, quarreling, loss of happiness, and eventual capitulation if someone decided to stay on at the company. Many times he suggested a sibling to leave. It wasn't always the best financial decision, but sometimes one's health demanded it. Sallie proved no exception. Everything he suspected was happening.

Ever since her brother stopped taking his medication he had become a different person; he never used to be this way, she said. Nowadays, however, she detested him, argued frequently, and resented his dismissal of her feelings. She also pointed out his condescending attitude. "I hate how he patronizes me. I don't know him anymore, and I'm pretty sure he's lost his mind," she said, exasperated beyond belief. She loathed his pretentious remarks and his constant interjections into how she did her work. Tom's eyes widened when she told him that he had signed her up for classes. That was actually a new one for him.

"I see," he said, trying to keep his composure.

"I can't stand him. He acts like he's the owner, and believes only his ideas count!" She then went on to describe a few examples including Tony's spending habits which corroborated with what Barb had said; this was why he met everyone separately. It allowed for free expression of feelings and truth. "It's like he doesn't get it. This company isn't his personal ATM!"

He nodded. Then met with Arthur. Normally, he only met with family members, but Barb insisted. She had ever reason to expect he would one day be her son-in-law.

Although the meeting was short Tom learned a lot about Arthur. He was sincere, highly efficient, valued others and their ideas, and genuinely tried to grow the company through driven-orientated strategies; he was modest, extending credit to others before himself, but accountable for both success as well as defeat. He took calculated risks, weighing his options and consulting the advice of others before executing; he sought neither trophy nor public praise, but achieved for his own personal pride.

He was intrinsically driven, believing in the virtues of self-reliance; he needed no external motivation or incentive except the reward of meeting a challenge, and in this case it was growing a company; Arthur shared what he had done thus far, noting the hurdles of working with Tony, but also the efforts to work together. They argued as often as they shook hands in reconciliation or even hugged it out. But still there were clashes.

At Tom's asking, Arthur shared how Tony had become more physically aggressive towards him, shoving him against the wall; his head had barely missed a nail sticking out the wall. Other times there was just pushing, bullying, and intimidation.

"I see," said Tom, getting a better picture now; although violent behavior was not uncommon in these circumstances it certainly didn't excuse it.

Arthur went on, telling him how the two often collided over seemingly trivial things, such as in one case he was talking to an employee when Tony suddenly came barging over and demanded the employee stop talking and only listen to him and any orders he had to give.

"I was as surprised as the other employee," he said, "especially because the other employee was an intern I was training."

Tom's eyes widened more than he had with Sallie.

Then it was time to meet with Victor. But this proved easier said than done. Victor evaded him like the plague, and they had to continuously reschedule until Barb put her foot down; not a single employee was to ask for him until after he met with Tom.

And it was in this meeting that Tom learned that he wasn't the first coach the company had hired. He was in fact one of many, and frankly, this was largely why Victor didn't see any reason to talk with him. Why bother if he was just going to be another number.

Tom began. "What do you see as the strengths at this company?"

"My children."

"Could you explain? How so?"

Victor rolled his eyes impatiently. He was totally uninterested in doing this. "My daughter is learning the finances of the business, and my son is learning how to run things. Both are learning how to make important decisions. They make mistakes, but they're learning."

"Are there any weaknesses that you see?"

"None really. Everybody is doing their job."

As much as Tom wanted to share what the others had said he didn't. It was important to hear from each one without any bias tainting the views. "What about any opportunities? Are there any that you believe are helping grow this company."

"My son."

That was interesting. "Can you elaborate?"

"He's making decisions like an owner, some good, some bad, but he's learning."

"I see. And lastly, do you feel there are any threats to the company?"

Victor shook his head. "None, but then I'm retiring in a few years and so whatever happens after that is up to my children to figure out. They can do whatever they want with this company when I'm retired."

His eyes widened the biggest at that remark.

Chapter 46

Taking Steps Forward

Tom started to put his notes together, and to say the least he was amazed the company still had a beating heart. Now it was time to meet with Tony; he didn't necessarily save the best for last.

Tony treated it like a newscast interview. He laughed, smiled, and had a great time answering Tom in lengthy responses that surpassed any dissertation. He proudly lauded his talents, highlighted achievements, and took credit for any success the company had experienced. "What can I say," he said with a chuckle. "I was just born to be a CEO."

He enumerated on the company's strengths that not surprisingly all came back to him. He talked about his grandiose ideas, his change coalition, and how the team was beginning to embrace it, which was an interesting way to phrase years of failure. "When we come together we move as one," he said, using his hands expressively. "We're not there yet, but our culture is alive and very organic. It's growing every day and my job is to continue to shower it with water and keep it going."

"You're comparing the company to a plant?"

"Yes," he said jovially, loving the analogy. "I am the water and the soil and the sun is the warmth we feel when we reach higher with each success. It's a great feeling I got to tell you. I'm very excited."

He nodded, choosing to move on. "What about any weaknesses, or limitations?"

Tony crossed his legs, again taking his time and speaking almost like academia. "My mother. I love her, and I want her to grow as a person, but she's holding the company back from reaching its next step. There is so much potential in her and I want to help her get to that next level, but there are so many important decisions that need to be made, and I'm not sure she's ready or willing to make them."

"What kinds of decisions?"

"Well, it took her a long time to hire our new accounting firm, and even still she has yet to meet with them; you see that's what I'm talking about. This company needs leadership that knows what it wants and takes it. I love her, but she really needs to pick up the pace." The look of theatrics was as fabricated as his concern. "We are on a great path to success, but what hold us back are the people who don't wish to change; you can't just grow a company the same way you started it. If you want to grow then you have learn how to grow, and that means talking with other leaders, becoming more educated, taking classes, and being prepared to make hard decisions."

"What kinds of hard decisions do you mean?"

"Like cutting the fat from the lean."

Another analogy. "Explain what you mean."

"As the future leader of this company I know that some employees are better than others; it's just a fact of life. But you can't grow with professional helpers. You need people that are highly qualified, talented as well as reliable, and can do a job even under the most extreme conditions; everything I do at the company is meant to push others, and to help them discover their untapped potential.

"We can't have a future with mediocrity. It just won't happen. If you want to a twenty-five million dollar company than you have to start thinking like one, even if you're not there yet. How are things done differently? What policies or procedures need to change? What sort of hires should we be making? Are there any new qualifications that we need to be looking at?

"But most importantly is our leadership. We can't have indecisive leadership. There's no place for that in growth, and while I love my mother she's very indecisive. I have to push and push if we are to be successful."

He discussed his broad dreams for the company, its necessary leaps forward, and how he was becoming an expert in not just his industry but in growth. "You don't really need to become an expert in your field to grow something," he said. "You just need to innovate, and I am our company's innovator."

"I see. Well, are there any threats that you feel exist at the company that might hinder growth?"

"Yes, most definitely. I would say my father. We cannot move forward as a company without direction, and my vision is what gives this company that direction. My father, however, stagnates us. He really needs to retire along with my mother. They both fail to see the big picture and I'm afraid they aren't really ready to advance to the next stages of business growth. I'm very proud of them, but at this point they need to pass the torch onto something who has the will to take us to the next level."

"I see. Anything else?"

"Well, I'd like to return to discussing the unique opportunities we have at this company. For starters, few companies have a visionary, such as myself. It really helps to engrain in everyone a sense of purpose, direction, and resolve in facing the growing number of challenges ahead. We as a company can move mountains, but only if we are all onboard, and getting everyone onboard takes vision.

"Which brings me to my sister and her boyfriend. They are both fantastic and resourceful, but they don't know yet how to take directions well; it's a learning curve, but some of us are not born natural leaders. You understand? You've met many CEOs and I'm certain some of your clients have experienced similar examples of family members that believe they should be a part of the executive team when really they shouldn't.

"I see."

"It's just natural for someone to believe they are worthy of the caliber of being called CEO, or think they have the wherewithal to guide a company; its silly I know, but some people just think they're as talented as individuals like me. But what can I say? I do what I must, because I'm a visionary. I have a constant flurry of ideas and I need people to act on them without delay; when people ask questions it only holds us back.

"After all, vision is about being organic. It's about taking risks as well as accepting the fact that feelings will get hurt. It's nothing personal, just business; if I have to cut the fat than that's the way it is. A person shouldn't be insulted by the fact he or she was fired. Instead, they should look at it as a challenge to do better next time. At our company, we hire slow fire fast. That's our belief, and it creates a very positive atmosphere of growth. Like I said, it's all about being organic, developing others, and cultivating ideas, and I take immense pride in being able to blossom our company's ideas and growth."

Chapter 47

The One Page Plan

When a natural disaster suddenly hit the area Tony jumped on the opportunity to start up a charity to help those in need. He later admitted that his real intent was actually to capitalize on the sufferings of others; he just couldn't pass up the chance to be in the limelight.

* * * * * * * * *

Once Tom had finished meeting with everyone he assembled the team offsite, away from the company. The purpose of this was two-fold. First, a different location meant less distractions and secondly to impress upon the team that a company should be able to function without its leadership. "If your business suffers in your absence then something is wrong."

When Arthur stepped in Tony took offense. "And what is he doing here?" he asked, as if he were an expert on leadership development. "A leadership team should be limited to four or less. I don't think he should be here or even wait outside; he's not part of this family and I think it would jeopardize the integrity of the meeting if someone were eavesdropping." He ordered Arthur back to the office. "Go bring in sales like I've asked you to do." He turned to Tom. "It's so hard to get good help these days."

Tom gave him a faint smile. "Actually, if I'm not mistaken, Barb requested his presence."

Tony turned to her with the most horrified look upon his face, as though she had just blasphemed. "You can't be serious. He's not family."

"I asked him and so he's here. Let it go," she said.

Tony felt personally insulted. How had his energy and confidence inspired such corrosive heresy? He didn't understand his mother, and made it clear during the meeting that this exemplified yet again what he had said in his meeting with Tom. She was making unwise decisions.

But Tom moved on, distributing the meeting's agenda and starting with some basics. First and foremost, he discussed the rules. This was meant to be a productive use of everyone's time. That being said, everyone surely had opinions, so being professional was paramount; if at any time he felt the conversation needed to shift directions he would facilitate that. "Now let's begin with the first point that Barb has asked us to discuss."

First on the list was Joe. During her discussion with Tom she had elaborated on Joe, his pay, his forty hours plus overtime, and how it was costing her greatly to keep him; she wanted to renegotiate his pay. After all, Tony had no business signing any document without her consent. To say the least, she was outraged.

"I never agreed to this and I want it changed."

But Tony refused. "We need the best people in the industry, and if you decide to cut somebody off at their ankles after you hire then what message does that send, not to mention how it hurts their livelihood. If our employees can't move forward in their own personal success then how can we expect the company to move forward?

"The fact is he is a hard worker and we should be rewarding him, not hurting him, or else he may leave and how does that help up? We can't isolate our employees, mom. We have to develop them. I've visited many other companies, networked with CEOs, and educated myself on how we need to change if we expect to grow; knifing somebody does nothing but incur their resentment, and I'm trying to develop a culture of growth. So not only would you be hurting Joe, but also me as well as everyone else who has benefited from our cultural growth."

"And just exactly what am I supposed to post his costs against? You tell me!" She was instantly livid; months of caged animosity vented then. "I can charge clients for his forty hours, but if we have a slow week then what am I supposed to bill his overtime to? You tell me. Since you think you've got all the answers mister, you tell me!"

"Mother," he said patiently, his tone patronizing. "You're blaming me but all I've done is tried to help you. I have brought countless accounting firms to you over the years but instead of considering them you simply rejected them. How can I build a growth culture if you can't get our finances in order."

She slammed her hand on the table. "This is not about me. I've been running this company for thirty years. I know what I'm doing."

He fired back. "You and dad have done a great job of starting this company, but you don't know how to take it to the next level and pretending like you do is only hurting us. I'm sorry if you feel my decisions are mistaken, but I've done my research and I know how to guide us; what you and dad need to do is let me take over. As I've said countless times, I know how to guide us. You just have to trust that your son can in fact do it."

"You haven't earned my trust yet."

"So what? You listen to Sallie and him, is that it?" he said, pointing to Arthur. "They've been taking direction from me, and yet somehow they get the credit. How does that make sense?"

Sallie jumped in, firing back, rejecting his overture that her success was entirely owed to his divinity. "Can't you just listen for once, or our you so stuffed up in the head that you can't see how stupid some of your ideas are? You don't have to clean up your messes, but I do!"

He shook his head. "I am the visionary of this company, and I work very hard to build our future by networking and preparing us for expansion."

She cut him off. "Expansion! What are you talking about? You have single-handedly crippled us!"

"Not even close. I have introduced company culture where none existed before. I have put us on a path of growth, and inspired others to take the initiative. Look at where we were before to where we are now."

"Yeah, we're in a more shittier position. The only reason why there's sales coming in is because of Arthur, not you. But if you need to take credit for his ideas then go for it, because frankly I'm sick of you and your bullshit!"

"His sales strategy came from talking with me!"

"Then it's your idea! Are you happy? It's yours now can we move on with the meeting," she crossed her arms in disgust.

"What have I said that's offensive," Tony said, pushing her buttons even more. "All I've done is help grow this company, but if that's not what anyone wanted then go right ahead and blame me for all the problems."

"Nobody's blaming you. Stop pretending you're the victim here. You're not! You don't bring in sales and when you do everything goes to crap, and then mom and I have to figure out how to pay for your stupid mistakes."

He shook his head in disbelief. "Honestly, I have no idea what you're talking about. Maybe it's just your time of the month."

"Okay, yeah, it's my time of the month. Excuse me," she said to the group and stormed out. Victor followed, but not to console her but rather to take a phone call. He was happy to have any reason to leave.

For a moment there was awkward silence. Arthur remained quiet, refraining from giving his opinion. After all, it was a family quarrel. Until he was married he felt it best to remain diplomatic; Tom gave the group a ten-minute break, allowing tensions to subside. Clearly, there was a lot of pent-up anger.

When they came back Tom resume the discourse. "What's clear to me is that nobody is on the same page. I believe that's a fair statement to make. So our goal then is to start with that. What I want to introduce you to this afternoon is something we call a one-page plan. This will help you all move closer together."

Tony had read about that and clapped his hands, but Tom ignored his flattery. "So, let's begin with your company core values," he said. "Now, by a show of hands if I were to ask any employee at your company what the core values were would anyone know?" Only Tony raised his hand. "I see. Well, let me first start with a basic question. What are core values?"

Tony happily answered, elaborating on them as the keystones of any business. "They define a company, and become your tools for hiring as well as firing." In fact, he had tried many times to impart core values upon the company, but his strong-armed approach had only mired its acceptance.

"How many should we have," Barb asked Tom.

"No more than six, but no fewer than three."

After several hours of debate, the team polished down a list of five words that most closely defined the company: Work Ethic, Team Player, Promoting Growth, Proactive, and Resourceful.

"I want to add one more," Tony said. "Spirited. I believe that our culture is about bringing passion to what we do." But Tom hesitated to add it.

"Spirited is too subjective," he cautioned. Core values had to be as objective as possible. "Can you really fire somebody for not being spirited enough?"

Tony nodded. Of course he could.

Chapter 48

Reluctant Choices

For hiring Tom, the price tag was $54,000 a year, and he met with the team once a month for six hours. This equated to being $4,500 a month, or a rate of $750 an hour.

* * * * * * * * *

Although the meeting had initially started with Joe it hadn't finished it; Tom tabled it after seeing how heated the issue was. Barb didn't mind. She not only liked Tom's direction but also the coach himself; he wasn't like the others in the past. He wasn't afraid to stand up to her son. He neither acquiesced to Tony's lofty ideas nor became blinded by his zealous vision. Perhaps even more important was his blunt nature; whereas others in the past had edited their speech Tom didn't.

He said it like he saw it, and one of first priorities in addition to the core values was tackling who had the final decision. At the moment, Barb and Victor both had it, but in their own respective ways; if it was financial the final say went to Barb. In all other matters it went to Victor. Tom put a stop to this. "There cannot be two leaders if you indeed wish to grow," he said. "Don't get me wrong. What you've been doing has worked, but if you choose to go down this road of growth, beyond three million dollars, you will need to pick between the two of you. And if I may I'm going to advocate for Barb, because nothing happens unless you have cash and that's what she's in charge of."

It was put to a vote and to everyone's surprise Victor happily consented. In hindsight this made total sense, because of how often he evaded problems. Thus, Barb became CEO and had final say over all business affairs; the only one twisting in his seat was Tony.

"Well, now that we have that out of the way onto the next course of business," the coach said, pulling up the agenda. They were now onto financial reporting, and Tony quickly jumped in. He had quite a lot to say. "Tom, let me just say that as this company's sales manager I need to have a one-page report on my desk every morning so that I can see where we stand as a company today, where it was yesterday, and where we need to be tomorrow. Only then can I make the critical decisions for us to grow."

Before Tom could speak Barb fired back. "If you're the sales manager then how come you don't have the numbers? I can't do anything without your numbers."

"Mother, this isn't about you or me. It's about all of us growing together. I need your report so that I can measure how my team is doing, and whether they need to pick up the pace." For five minutes the two went back and forth until Tom finally intervened.

Unexpectedly, and to everyone's surprise, he took Tony's side. "He does raise a good point, so I have to agree with him. A sales manager needs as much information as he can to make the best possible decisions." Barb was stunned. She was in disbelief and about ready to fire him; how he could suddenly reverse his course and sail to the wind of her son? But to add insult to injury, he then agreed with Tony's next point that he should be in charge of Human Resources.

Chapter 49

Bitterness

Interestingly enough, Barb had voted for her husband to be CEO as had Tony. Meanwhile, Sallie and Tom had voted for her, which meant the deciding vote came down to Arthur. He picked her, and Tony never forgave him.

* * * * * * * *

Tony couldn't believe his luck. All of a sudden Tom was on his side; was the coach becoming a believer? He wasn't sure, but remained optimistic; over the next month he shined, parading down the hallway and flaunting his newfound victories; per Tom, he received a report each and every morning, much to the disgust of his mother and sister; arrogantly, he required it be delivered in person.

Barb refused and put the burden on Sallie, who in turn tried to put it on someone else in accounting, but Tony rejected it unless it came from either her or Barb; in case he had questions he required someone to answer his inquiries right there and then.

"Then pick up the phone and call someone."

"Sallie, my time is very precious and I can't be running around trying to find answers when it's just easier for you or mom to be here."

"My time is just as important."

He shook his head. "Actually it's not. Without sales you wouldn't have a job."

"Then why don't you sell instead of hanging around here all day! Why is Arthur doing all the selling?"

"He's not. In fact, he does very little compared to me, and besides all of his leads come from me. So without me he wouldn't be able to sell. So as you can see, my time is far more valuable than either you or him."

And so, each day Sallie brought him his report. But he made her wait. Many times he was on the phone, and refused her inside until he was done; the fact that he had a lock didn't stop her from banging. Once, he made her wait twenty minutes; he asked for the report at 8 AM, then 7:30, 7:00, and by the end of the month it was 6:30 AM.

"Teamwork is about everyone doing what I say," he said, having no shame about the smirk on his face.

Throughout the month, he flaunted his triumphs as often as he demeaned his sister, pointing out her flaws; he belittled Amanda, who worked in Accounts Receivable. He insulted them daily, whether in person or email; he pointed out their weight issues, criticizing Sallie for being a bit overweight; he was one to talk. He was obese.

"I wouldn't say it if it wasn't true," he said, trying to justify his hateful words in the name of love. "I only want you to grow." If her self-esteem was shaky before it collapsed under the weight of his horrible words; when she tried to throw it back at him he dismissed it, alleging it wasn't the same thing. Whereas he claimed her words were simply vengeful he said he was trying to motivate her.

He then enrolled her into more college classes. "It's not that you're becoming educated," he said, "It's that you're learning how to do what I ask better."

He then put the newly instituted core values to the test by firing two technicians for demonstrating what he called a "lack of spirit." It was a pitiful display of leadership. With the emergency service calls most if not all of the crews were working long 14-hour days; with their weekends gone there was now no room to relax. But as sacrificial lambs the message was clear. Work to death or be fired.

By the end of the month there was no love for Tony in the entire company. Everyone hated him; whatever culture he had tried to impress the last few years was cast aside; his belittling had earned him no favors; his tyranny in scheduling technicians was as resented as his liberal interpretation of the core values; but what infuriated his mother most of all was his absence of sales.

By the end of the month he had achieved very little and to everyone's surprise he announced he had spent the entire month developing a company on the side; Barb was exasperated. She couldn't contain her anger and in one of the longest, loudest fights she had it out with her son.

"It is what it is," he said, putting his hand in her face. "I am the living embodiment of Spirited." On the company's dime he earned $100,000 for his enterprise while earning next to nothing for his parents.

Chapter 50

The Drill Sergeant

Many times, Tony admitted to masturbating to the thought of firing employees. "Just the thought of it gives me goose bumps," he said excitedly.

* * * * * * * *

At the next month's meeting Tony walked in jubilantly. It had been an amazing month; like a kid getting every present on his wish list, he entered the room with a huge smile; if he could keep this momentum going he was certain to replace his mother as CEO in no time.

Tom first thanked everyone for coming. Then he began by taking a pulse of how everyone felt the company was doing. Only Tony responded positively; although the company had done well in sales, just above $285,000, this was only slightly better than the previous month; Tom was puzzled. It was good news, but he expected the company to have done a bit better than that.

"Let's see the breakout," he said, asking Tony to pull out his laptop with the monthly spreadsheet. It contained all sales figures. As they scrolled down the list everyone could see how each salesperson had done, from Antonio to Victor, Arthur to the senior estimator as well as Tony; when it came to the latter Tom said to stop. His jaw dropped. Tony's numbers were abysmal.

"Why are your numbers so low," he asked, quite surprised. Whereas everyone else was in the ballpark of fifty thousand dollars Tony had only achieved a paltry $500! Tom turned to him. "Care to explain?"

Anyone else might have crawled into the fetal position, but not Tony. He was too proud of what he had done to feel any sense of defeat. "We're a team, and as a team we did very well. We reached our monthly goal, and so I'd say we actually had a successful month."

"The company certainly pulled its weight, but I wouldn't count you in that. Just over $285,000 and all you have to show for that is $500. I mean that's ridiculous!"

"Well, as the sales manager my job is to distribute leads and make sure they are followed up on. I'm not responsible for generating revenue. That's my team's job."

"Since when? The role of a sales manager is to generate revenue. You sell, manage, and report. That's what that role entails." He looked to Barb. "Am I wrong?"

She couldn't agree more.

But Tony wouldn't be shamed. He started to defend himself, clarifying definitions, and interpreting his role as visionary, but Tom had had enough. He cut him off, and threw Tony into a bowl of humiliation.

"She pays you a salary every month- and a reasonably nice one at that- and in return all you give her is $500! What kind of a sales manager are you? Seriously, how can you sit there and defend your actions when there is a company on the line here? This figure is appalling. I'm disgusted at it, and no doubt she's disgusted by it too. There is no excuse for this, absolutely none. It's pathetic!"

Tony remained poised; he still wanted those clients of his. "I distribute the leads that became revenue, so therefore I receive credit for those sales too. Thus, I actually contributed to our final number much more than just $500."

But Tom wouldn't let that fly. "How much then?"

"What do you mean?"

"If you're telling us that you receive credit for the leads to become sales then how much of that revenue are you claiming? Are you saying that your leads contributed to ten percent of that $285,000, or are you saying that 50% of all those sales came from your leads, or are you claiming all of them? Which is it?"

"I'm afraid I don't have those figures."

"Aren't they on there?" he said, pointing to the laptop. "Isn't that what you use every day?" This was just insulting; Tom had lost all patience with him. Here he was trying to claim the hard work of others as his own.

"I contribute with leads," he said, deferring to repetition, but Tom refused to accept that.

"Unless you can prove how much your leads contributed then I'm going to take your $500, and I'm going to say shame on you. Shame on you for wasting your everyone's time here. This is not only pathetic, but an absolute shame to anyone who calls himself a sales manager." Barb smiled from across the table.

Chapter 51

The Opportunity

Tom called for a break; he was simply too appalled to keep going. Pulling Barb aside he invited her to his firm's executive summit; it was something he did for all of his clients. Every year, his client-owners traveled to a spa resort to spend the week sharing their thoughts and relaxing. It was a nice retreat, and a way for his firm to say thank you. "This would be great for you and Victor to get away and have some fun. I'm sure a vacation for you both is long overdue."

Barb happily agreed and once the meeting resumed it was announced. At once, Tony objected; how he had the audacity to think he deserved it after his pitiful show of numbers was beyond anyone's comprehension, but he insisted that as the visionary of the company he should have had been offered the opportunity first.

Tom wasn't surprised. "You need to get your numbers up first," he said unconditionally.

But Tony refused to let it go. "There's a lot that I do at this company, from marketing to building culture. We are a company driven towards growth, and I have been at the forefront of that change since the beginning, and it is with that in mind that any direction this company takes in growing or building culture should have my stamp of approval on it. Therefore, I look forward to attending this summit in my mother's place. I'm sure she will understand how important it is that we move forward together, and build a strong family unit in the process."

Barb scoffed at that. "You show me the numbers first, and then we'll see who goes."

"Mother," he added, "I have helped in numerous ways to take this company to the next level. My attention every month is about growing. Sales generation is the responsibility of the team, not just one person. So, you can't hold me accountable to all the numbers. That's not how business works.

"I generate leads through networking, so while I don't have the figures in front of me I certainly contributed to the overall count for this month; just because I don't have the numbers doesn't mean a thing. That number of

$285,000 is because of me, and I did that while developing a business on the side as well as networking.

"You can pretend all you want that I didn't do a thing this month, but that's simply not true. I work harder than anyone at this table, because I want you to reach your dream of getting passed three million dollars. All of dad's leads came from me, and he and Antonio earned business because I qualified those leads.

"And instead of giving credit to Arthur for his sales you should be giving that credit to me, because it has been my sales approach that has eliminated the poor salesmen we had, prepared the new spreadsheets, and filtered all of our business. You're giving him credit, but he has only been doing what I tell him to do.

"But if you and dad and everyone at this table think that I haven't been doing a thing then fine. Go ahead and believe that, but nobody here deserves that retreat more than me. I've worked harder than anyone else; I'm at the office before everyone, and I'm the last to leave. Since I started I've done so much to improve the culture and sales of this company, but not you or dad will accept that. Maybe it's because you still can't accept me for who I date, maybe? But I know how to take this company to the next level, and frankly, when I'm CEO not you or dad will get in my way."

It was as insulting as it was a lie. But Barb knew better than to believe anything he said; his words were nothing but propaganda and fibs. "You're not going."

Dreams and Wishes

<u>Chapter 52</u>

Playing God

Because of her brother's hateful words about her weight, Sallie fell into a deep depression. Only with Arthur's help did she recover. Together they went to the gym and did yoga, and in six months she had sculpted her body into a beautiful hourglass.

* * * * * * * *

Until the second they entered the airport Tony continued to shame her for denying him what he called an opportunity to grow; he still insisted he had more right to go to the spa than they did. And the second they left he began running the company like it was his own.

At once, he ordered technicians to report to work an hour earlier than usual. Now they were coming in at 4

AM, most with only less than five hours of sleep and no family time. But if anyone thought coming in earlier meant leaving early he was sorely mistaken; Tony kept them out longer, giving them not just one emergency service call, but as many as three; now they were finishing after midnight.

"The only way this company will grow is when everyone steps up," he said, rejecting their protests. He worked them up to 20 hours a day, and to further add fuel to the fire he ignored the rotation cycle Arthur had created; what need was there for rotation when everyone should be on call, thought Tony.

He leveraged the core values against any protests, terminating four technicians in his father's absence for allegedly underperformance. "You should want to grow," he said, relishing his newfound sense of authority. He then dismissed two warehouse helpers that were recently hired; he then insisted that Troy supervise all crews, not just one.

Frank put his foot down. Enough was enough. The crews were fatigued, and while Troy had begun to show promise as a leader he was in way prepared to manage all of the crews. "I cannot allow you to continue this," he said. "These men are the blood of this company and you have no right pushing them this way."

Tony smirked. "Actually, I can. I have every right to do as I please. I have the full support of the union, and if you have a problem with that then you can find somewhere else to work, but I won't let you prevent this company from moving forward."

"Moving forward? How! You're overworking these men. They're exhausted! Open your eyes."

Tony called an immediate companywide meeting to reinforce his role as heir apparent and de facto CEO in his mother's absence. He made it crystal clear that anyone trying to object or interfere with his orders would be in direct violation of the core values, which he alleged were tied to his vision and subsequently his orders; he spelled it out. Failure to adhere to the core values- by his definition- constituted insubordination, and he defined the core values how he saw fit.

"When everyone listens to me and obeys then we move forward and grow together," he said, dismissing two interns and another technician in order to show how serious he was; he claimed they had failed to show spirit. And then in a final inexplicable act, he moved Joe into sales. Why he did this nobody knew, but it not only came as a surprise to the company, but also to Joe.

He was a technician. That was what he knew how to do; his coworkers and customer's spoke very highly of him, and he could upsell wonderfully. So why Tony thought it was a marvelous idea to move him was beyond anyone's logic.

Chapter 53

Improving Sales Numbers

In addition to moving Joe into sales, Tony gloated that he would, not could, book $35,000 in just one day!

* * * * * * * *

After his setback in the leadership meeting and his denial to the spa resort, Tony went about ensuring no such incident occurred again; he didn't look at it like defeat, but rather that his efforts hadn't been visible enough. And so, forgoing profit, he instead focused entirely on revenue; if Tom wanted to see numbers then that's what he would give him. He booked an $83,000 deal at a margin of 14% ($11,620), but then lost half of it through his persistent negligence and interference with operations.

He then won a contract worth $135,000, but at an even lower margin, and again lost most of the profit during the operation phase; he ultimately lost $45,000 on it. He booked another at a little over $32,000, but then failed to account for certain minor yet important details that resulted in total profit loss. Contract after contract was the same, but all that mattered to him was the amount on the contract.

He matched competitor's prices, failed to measure, overpromised but under-delivered, and turned all customer complaints over to his mother to handle; one might think he was digging his own grave by doing so, but he always pointed the finger. Thus, any loss was somebody else's fault. Even a small project of $8,700 lost a considerable amount and someone lost a job over it.

He further erred in his estimates, failing to account for any contingencies, which resulted in additional losses as well as more headaches for those in operations; he compounded their problems and migraines were only the beginning. Even simple calculations were neglected that created colossal problems, such as the time when he bid labor for one day when it took four; he failed to measure properly, ruining an almost $30,000 order; he had the wrong product ordered, or did it late, or not even at all.

And all the while he belittled the operations team, challenged their expertise, and exasperated their efforts to make any profit by his constant interference of rescheduling technicians to other work, firing technicians, or sabotaged their efforts; his "All Hands In" companywide meeting dragged on for hours and became the bane of everyone's existence. Those that tried to confront him were let go; those that caught his mistakes were let go, and those that ignored the mistakes and lost money were let go. It was a no-win scenario. But Tony still prided himself as living the core values, especially being a team player.

Chapter 54

Nervousness

The natural disaster immobilized the area, ruining homes and devastating families. "When we come together as a community," said Tony, soliciting support to his movement, "we grow together."

* * * * * * * * *

It took Joe nearly three months to book $35,000. Tony had promised everyone that he could pull it off in less than that, but whatever resources or training he might have given him to be successful were withheld. "This is about you finding your potential," he told him.

He denied him any training or even guidance on how to network, but that didn't stop him from being sent to one event after the next; trade shows, golf outings, dinner banquets, conferences, speakers, any and all sorts of networking events Joe attended, learning the ropes very slowly. He asked Tony to join him, but he refused. "I have my own networking events I attend, but just because I can't go doesn't mean you can't walk out of there with leads." He not only expected Joe to get leads, but also fifty of them!

When Tony refused to go Arthur went instead. He showed him how it was done; a big part of networking was being yourself, but also finding something to help others remember you by. For Arthur, it was his adventures; his stories were unparalleled. In fact, so unique were they that he won many contracts that way, everything from his travels to the jobs that he held in the past. They were just so different; although they worked together and Joe got a better sense of networking he still felt distraught.

"I still feel uneasy," he said. "I'm a technician, not a salesman. I love what I do, but this selling is really hard. I'm really worried here." Aware of Tony's purging habit he had every right to be perturbed, but as Arthur soon learned Joe had even more reason to worry. Apparently, Tony was feeding him cold leads. "Every lead he gives me is a dead-end. Either the customer has already bought from someone else, or it's a lead that weeks old."

Arthur assured him he was look into it.

"Thanks man. I owe you one."

Upon further investigation, it was discovered that not only were Tony's leads to him cold, but also his reason. He was too busy promoting his new charity! For whatever reason he valued his public relations charity over improving sales. When confronted, Tony argued his job was simply to distribute leads, not pursue them. That was the job of the salesman. So, if the lead was cold then it was Joe's fault.

<u>Chapter 55</u>

A Hard Worker

Because of the natural disaster, Victor and Barb were delayed until the airport was repaired. Of course, they didn't mind a few extra days at the spa.

* * * * * * * *

Joe was a superb technician. Praised by both his fellow technician and clients alike, he was dedicated and passionate about his work. He delivered quality, and could be relied upon when working independently. Invaluable as a team member the crews respected him, and crew leaders bartered for him, often making trades to get him for the day; although every technician was valued, Joe was a rare gem. He was eager to learn, had a strong work ethic, and was not a prima donna unlike some of the other techs.

Even repeat customers asked for Joe. One client even refused to sign a contract until he had Victor's word that he would be on the project; personable as well as friendly, Joe often showed clients his progress for the day, showing them how to work something that was technical, and often giving them a schedule of when he might finish.

This not only pleased clients but also encouraged repeat business. Thus it was that Joe earned the company far more as a technician than as a salesman; without him, things began to fall apart: promised deadlines passed, clients became upset, and blame was spread. The weight passed from one person to the next, and in one instance a client became so incensed that he canceled the project outright. It had been worth $45,000.

Chapter 56

The Argument

Despite Arthur's help Joe still felt troubled. He barely slept and felt that each day was going to be his last at work. "Why can't I just be a tech? I make the company more money doing it!" But Tony refused his pleas. "It is what it is," he said coldly.

* * * * * * * *

Unlike his pitiful $500 a month ago, Tony had now booked just over $188,000; it had been a month of despotism and everyone was glad to have Victor and Barb back. As the executive team met with Tom, Tony proudly showed off his results, lauding everything he had done in his parent's absence as though it were proof enough for him to take over.

When it came time to discuss the numbers he again claimed everyone's leads as part of his number; arguing was pointless. Tony took credit for all of Joe's efforts, meaning that everything he had done were null and void and thus, on paper, Joe had done nothing. He tried to claim his father's, Antonio's, the senior estimator's and even Arthur's numbers, but Tom stopped him. How could he possibly take credit for everybody's efforts?

"It is what it is," Tony replied, seeing no reason to not take credit. He had distributed leads and felt entitled to take a percentage of that success; if that meant taking all the credit then so be it.

Tom disputed that. It was one thing to take credit for the distribution of leads, but to take credit for the end result was not appropriate. "If you actively participated in the sale process from start to finish then I would agree with you, but you've only distributed the leads, nothing more."

The two went back and forth, accomplishing little until Tom simply refused to accept it. "Your mother pays me so until the day you pay me I will go by what she wants to do." She acknowledged his distribution. Nothing more.

Tony became exasperated.

"Look at this past month. I took the reins while the two of you were away and led our company to a successful month. On top of that I am proud to say I have been leading the charge in our public relations by promoting a charity to help those in need. To say that I don't deserve the credit for all the sales is ridiculous when I'm the sales manager."

She interrupted him. "But a sales manager is responsible for sales, not for taking credit of everyone else's efforts. You do your part and they do theirs, and you report to me on those numbers."

He shook his head in disagreement. "No mom, that's not how it works. Sales managers are responsible for the distribution of leads, the recording of sales, and the efforts of the team. Since I am managing the team I get credit for what they accomplish, just as you get credit for the accomplishments of the company as a whole."

"Yes, but I don't take credit for what your father does. He does his job and I do mine."

"Then you don't understand the role of a CEO. Being a CEO and visionary means being able to take credit for everyone else's work, because they believed in your vision. That's why CEOs are paid so much, because they inspire people into action. It's only fair then that they take credit for their inspiration."

"You need to be doing your work and nothing more. If you would have spent more time selling instead of on this charity you could have brought in more sales"

"Again mother, you miss the point of what it means to be a CEO."

"Oh, then enlighten me," she said sarcastically.

"There's no need for attitude. I'm happy to share with you how public relations are important to the growth of a company."

"Your father already has a reputation. There's no need to promote the business anymore."

"Can you let me finish? I was trying to explain how public relations help grow our business, because it connects leaders in our community and opens up the possibility of leads generation."

"But you're not selling! How does it sell?"

"You need to let me finish."

"No, this is stupid. You need to be out selling. That's how this company grows! Not with some charity scheme."

"Mother, companies are not just about numbers. They are about projecting meaning into our lives. We have to stand for people, not just a product or service. I am trying to build a change coalition that will take us to the next level, because we are a company that's more than just metrics. We are about real, living, breathing people, and I want to show that off to the world, because when we do that people will see we are more than just a company. We are human. We care. We are givers who care about our community; we're not just takers out for profits.

"We need to stand for a cause. We have to be an inspiration, a leader, and that starts with helping those in need. It's the only way to go to the next step; we have to be open with our community. We have to be active with it, and engage its needs. That's what being a leader in this next step is all about, but if you're not ready to do that then we can't grow. We need that go-getter as a leader. I'm that go-getter.

"If you and dad continue to do the same thing as you've done in the past then we won't grow; its just fact. The only way this company is going to grow is by passing the torch to me. I see where we need to go. I'm already taking us there. I just need for you two to retire."

"Well we're not. Not yet."

"And that's fine, but understand until you do we can't grow. Sallie can't grow us and neither can Arthur. Only I know how to do it." She started to speak, but he went on. "That's why I'm pushing things on you. I got you a new accounting firm, Tom as our coach, and why we will be hosting the charity at this company."

"You're not hosting anything here. You didn't get my permission to do it."

"I don't need your permission to help us grow."

"I forbid anybody from helping you."

"That's not being a team player, and last I checked that's a core value of ours- and as Tom said, core values are what we use to hire and fire."

The connotation was not lost on anyone. It was clear as day what he was doing. Tony was leveraging the core values to oblige their consent and participation.

"How dare you force me to agree," Barb said.

"You like everyone else agreed to the core values. I'm just enforcing what we discussed. After all, what good are core values if we don't live by them."

"How dare you!"

But it got worse. Tony intended to volunteer everyone at the company by leveraging the core values to get them to give up their weekend; since the technicians were already sitting by the phone Tony just figured it was easier to have them at the company in case a call came in. He saw no wrong in taking them away from their families.

"Everyone is invited," he said, being loose with the last word. "They can even bring their families along. It'll be a lot of fun."

As much as Tom wanted to argue there was little room for debate; nothing was negative. Since the union had agreed to Tony's demands the company didn't have to pay overtime on the weekends; the core values were being applied, although liberally; the charity event didn't necessarily cost anything, especially if lunch for the volunteers was donated; leads from the charity were a real possibility, and lastly Tony's numbers were up. Overall, it was a win-win despite any disgruntlement.

Chapter 57

Cash Flow

In the final quarter of that year, Tony earned just over $400,000 and yet his net profit was only $32,000. In sharp contrast, the senior estimator did almost $340,000 at 28% margin (over $92,000). Nevertheless, Tony awarded himself as the top salesman.

* * * * * * * * *

At $40 an hour, Tony now devoted the majority of his time to promoting his charity. He continued to book sales but remained as negligent as ever on his estimates and project management; he didn't care about the profit, only the revenue. Barb tried to protest, but he simply blew her off, dismissing her allegations as those of a generation that had lost touch with the times.

In three months he had a roller coaster ride of leadership meetings, up, down, and back up; triumphant, rejected, and then victorious once again, he had discovered that all he needed was to book revenue and nobody said a word. Now he was motivated. And at once, he began a new campaign of revamping the company's technology.

"Neither you nor dad know how to use a smart phone," he said, insinuating that the ability to text was somehow related to running a company. "And dad can't even use a computer!" Perhaps he had a point.

But in revamping, he fired the company's Information Technology (IT) Manager, hailed himself a pioneer of technology and locked all the passwords in his office, refusing to share any unless he felt so inclined; he badgered his father to buy smart phones for every employee as well as smart pads to showcase pictures to potential clients; pictures said a thousand words and easily sold.

He further dominated sales meetings, lecturing on the innumerable advantages of social media, going on and on about how great they were and how Antonio and the senior estimator needed to catch up with the times; they were as old school as Victor, except that they knew how to use a computer.

"Where the trend is going," he said, "the new search engine will not be Google. The new search engine will be social media where Facebook will have its own search – it already does- has a search engine where you search specific products, who of your friends have bought those products, what friends have talked about those products, and what local companies sell those products. We will be going away from Google, who is trying to stay alive, because younger people are moving away from Google, younger than Sallie. They are using social media to search for things they want to buy."

The senior estimator looked confused. His reply typified the older sentiment of the company. "What's the difference between Facebook and Google?"

"Facebook is social. That's where your friends are. Google is just a search engine."

"My friend lives two houses down from me."

"Not like that," he said. "Facebook is a place where everyone's friends can meet on the Internet, be social, share new finds, and update others on new things in their lives."

"What like getting married?"

"Exactly, or what cereal you ate for breakfast."

"Who the hell cares what I ate for breakfast?"

"But just that it. That's what people are doing."

"So, you want us to start using Facebook to share with others what we ate for breakfast? I mean I'll do it, because it's easier to get paid for that then actually bidding."

After several failed sales meetings Tony was told by Tom to just stick to the facts; as the saying goes, an old dog can't learn new tricks, so in lieu of obliging everyone to learn how to use social media like Facebook Tom suggested he hired an outside publicist to promote the company; if he had time between selling and promoting his charity then he could also utilize social media. Otherwise, sales meetings should be kept to the numbers.

As the date for the charity event neared, Tony began to leverage the core values against everyone's schedule. He started to volunteer others. "What is more spirited than giving your time to a cause greater than yourself," he said, thanking them as they mumbled under their breath. One employee had to forgo a wedding in which he was the best man. Another gave up a family reunion. Everyone resented Tony and the core values.

But to make matters worse, he then forced Barb and Sallie to empty the company's coffers. Holding the core values over their head he robbed the company of its cash to pay for "host paraphernalia," that included hiring a DJ, rigging up a giant American flag, and hiring a professional photographer to capture the moment.

"My heart cannot thank you enough," he said to them; there was now no money to pay the bills. "We are more than just a company. We are a family that stands for real, living, breathing people." Barb gave him the finger.

Chapter 58

Divine Right

As the charity event neared tensions rose; within a span of one week there were nearly two-dozen arguments between Barb and Tony; Sallie also argued with him, but every time he came out on top, refusing to be defeated. "This company needs a bold visionary, not somebody who should have retired five years ago," he said. Towards the end of the week one of the worst fights ever erupted. It began in the hallway between Sallie and him; the more she tried to explain the desperate situation the more he refused to listen.

"How is it my problem that you can't pay the bills," he said, playing innocent.

"Because you took it all you piece of shit!" She stormed into the company break room and began throwing napkins at him. "You're so fucking stupid!" They argued for ten minutes until she stormed outside, got into her car, and drove off. Tony would have raced after her but instead barged right into his mother's office. She was right in the middle of a meeting with Arthur, reviewing the company's finances.

"Get out and get selling," he said at him, shouting at the top of his lungs. "I am the visionary of this company, and I know what's best. My mother doesn't need you telling her what to do, and neither does my sister. Now do what I tell you and get out there!"

Barb snapped at him, ordering him to leave, but he refused, shutting the door behind him.

"This is my office and I want you out, so get out of here."

"Not before he does. He has poisoned this company, my sister, and you. I want him gone, and if you don't fire him then I will!"

"Why would I fire him or let you fire him when everything he has done has made this company money? You on the other hand have done nothing but sapped this company of every penny."

Tony's face smoked. He suddenly grabbed him by the shirt, opened the door, and threw him across the room. "I said do as I tell you! Now you're going to obey or else."

He picked him up from the floor and dragged him outside. He threw him onto the parking lot pavement, then jumped into his car, started the engine, backed out and then came forwards, aiming right for him.

Arthur recovered just in time to get out of the way. As he dodged him, Tony went straight into the flowerbed, destroying his mother's flowers and driving over bricks that ruined his car. "I am this company's future," he said, shouting from his window. "I will be a CEO, not you! This is a company car, and you just fucked it up by moving away. That's coming out of your pay!" Then he drove off. Later on he dismissed any allegation of possible assault and battery- if not voluntarily manslaughter- by saying, "I was simply helping him discover his untapped potential."

The following week he harassed his mother's department, barraging them with insults and defamation, slandering them to customers and to his network of business owners; there was no human resources to file a grievance with since he was given charge of that. And so, he had a free hand to say and do as he pleased.

Amanda got the worst. Everyday he called her fat. He insulted her attire, sent her hostile emails and even called her up on the phone shouting at her until she cried;

he gave her assignments outside of her responsibilities with unrealistic deadlines, such as superfluous reports that he didn't bother using but wanted done; he stood over her, dictating emails, letting her know what a terrible job she was doing; she went through at least two boxes of tissue a day and constantly turned to Arthur for help.

But day after day, he treated her unmercifully, belittling her just as much as he minimized her role; he treated her like his personal secretary and accused her of underperformance when she couldn't do his tasks and accounting; more than once he forced her to turn around in her seat and face him as he verbally abused her; she had to sit there and take it, because that was according to Tony what being a team player was all about. When she failed to read his mind he fired her for insubordination.

Chapter 59

The Capital Investor

Since he was in charge of Human Resources, Tony believed he had every right to hire and fire whoever he wanted. Five times he tried to fire his sister, but Barb hired her back every time. When he tried to fire his mother she just gave him the finger. Two hands.

* * * * * * * * *

Perturbed by Amanda's dismissal and fearing the worst for Joe, Arthur sought the advice of a close associate. The man happened to be a venture capitalist that gave him good insight into individuals like Tony. "Oh, I like him," he said, after Arthur briefed him. "But you have to understand why. In my line of work someone like Tony is profitable."

"How is that?"

"He makes me rich."

"Wait, how is that?"

The man explained. Someone like Tony was a shark. He had charisma, was magnetic, and could easily mobilize others into action. "These are idea people; these are movers and shakers. This is someone who sleeps two hours a night, because his mind is racing; there will be a million ideas before he even eats his breakfast- if he even has time for that. He's on the go. He has a flutter of ideas, and his brain rarely switch's off; he knows what he wants and he goes for it.

"There are few if any obstacles that block him from achieving his goals. He's got an idea and he thinks its golden; every idea in fact of his is brilliant and he's not about to rest and consider the details. He doesn't have time; he doesn't worry about the details, only the big picture.

"His ideas may not be, what's the word, complete, but his charisma sells it through. That's all it takes. If he can get people to invest and buy into his ideas that's all he cares about and that's all I care about, because when he fires up others my investment into someone like him pays off. I've invested millions over my career and live very comfortably as a result, but that's because I've put my faith into people like Tony. They are, I'm sorry to say to you, what this country needs; they are the babies of capitalism. They and capitalism go hand-in-hand; they are what economies need.

"That may seem like a bold statement, but these people who can start companies left and right, creating hundreds of new jobs in the process, and still not be tired. They're passionate, almost to the point of fanatical; they're driven and never slow down. My guess is that Tony is exactly this kind of person."

Arthur had to agree. It was.

"My advice to you is to allow this person to work. Let him do as he pleases; get out of his way. You will profit more than you know."

"But every decision of his costs us money."

"That may be," he said, "But trying to explain that to him isn't getting you anywhere is it? Remember, these personalities don't like to slow down. It's not that they're cold-hearted individuals. It's just that they aren't receptive to others criticism or hesitation; they want believers and followers."

"But he isn't logical."

"What is logical? To him, everything he is doing is logical. He has a certain picture in his mind and anything that blurs it only exasperates him."

"But he fired someone for not being able to read his mind. That's ridiculous."

"I couldn't agree more, but don't interfere."

"So you're saying I should just let him continue to make bad decisions that waste's the company's time and money with the hope that he'll actually help it grow?"

"Either that or get out. Sorry if that's not what you were expecting, but these people are not going to listen. Either you get out of the way or you simply follow. Those are your only two options."

He sighed. "What about if I was in a relationship, say with this person's sibling? If the three of us work at the same company couldn't we force this person out?"

"What, like if each of you owned a third of the business? Perhaps. But is that something the sibling is willing to live with; blood is thicker than water, so the more likely scenario is one sibling yielding to another more domineering one. That's far more probable."

"It sounds like this person always wins."

"Try not to think of it that way. Yes, his personality gets what he or she wants, but that's because they are too far ahead in the race to look back; they don't assimilate; they don't listen; they dictate through energy and charisma. It's their plan, their culture, their way."

"So either I accommodate or get out?"

"That's it. I won't sugarcoat it for you. Either let
Tony do as he wants or find another job, because in the end
he will be CEO. There is nothing that will stop it from
happening- short of him being fired- that you, his parents,
or this girl I suspect you're dating can do."

Chapter 60

The Grand Idealist

On the day of the charity event nearly 500 people participated. News channels broadcasted it, interviewing volunteers as well as Tony, who basked in the limelight. He greeted local politicians, other business owners, and stood beside the master of ceremony; over the microphone he thanked everyone for their support. "I can't thank you enough for coming out and showing your support. There is so much love here today!"

The master of ceremony had everyone give him a round of applause. "And I want to thank Tony now and *his* company for hosting this great event. We couldn't have done it without him or *his* team."

From a distance, Barb cringed her teeth and curled her fist into a hard ball. That son-of-a-bitch.

Chapter 61

The CEO

Tony felt euphoric. On a high, he had a great time, laughing, shaking hands, and loving the adulation; he pretended to be modest, but he savored the praise; for five hours he was the center of attention with a serotonin rush. "Everyone here has such a big heart," he said, joyfully. "I'm so glad we could share this day together."

When others thanked him for putting the event together he humbly smiled, claiming the idea of assembling food baskets as his own genius. It wasn't, but why not take credit for someone else's idea, especially when it involved ripping off copyrighted images and a banner? He later told Arthur that copyright infringement didn't matter. "I borrow good ideas to create something even greater. Besides, nobody sues a visionary."

Chapter 62

A Bright Sunny Day

It happened to be a perfect day to assemble food baskets outside. Everyone had a great time. There was music, food and the master of ceremony kept tally of how many baskets were prepared; the boy scouts were there as well as the girl scouts, other volunteer organizations, and Tony happily introduced them to *his* company, as the master of ceremony had so eloquently said.

He extended praise to the company's technicians for giving up their weekend; he publicly praised his mother and sister for giving up cash for entertainment; and he had the photographer be sure to capture every smile; Barb forced a smile as did Sallie. "As you can see, we are a company that embraces not just growth for ourselves, but our community as well. Thank you so much for coming."

He gave his mom a kiss on the cheek.

Chapter 63

Retaliation

Barb wiped it off. She had refused to participate, but Tony forced her. Now her weekend was ruined, and come Monday the phones would be ringing for why the bills hadn't been paid yet.

* * * * * * * *

The charity event was a huge success. Tony never felt more triumphant. He reveled in his victory, and shortly afterwards announced there would be a follow-up; he had aroused action and felt the momentum was too much to slow down. "We are now a movement," he said, inviting the community to set a new date; it was going to be an annual event now, and although twelve months away he started planning the next one.

Then without warning his world came crashing down. He stepped outside to see the furniture he had bought for the company's expansion in the dumpster; at once he lost his temper and barged into Barb's office.

"How dare you! Why would you set this company back? Look at what I've accomplished. Why would you prevent us from going to the next level?" His rage was uncontrollable and he brushed his hand across her desk, sweeping everything onto the floor. She feared for her life, but he was blocking the doorway. She ordered him out, but he refused until she admitted fault and gave up control of her department. "It's clear to me now that you are utterly and completely irresponsible with this company's future and money," he said, accusing her. "I'm getting dad to remove you from holding us back!"

She shot back. Victor would never kick her out.

"You WILL undo what you did!"

"I won't do a thing. There is no money to expand so I don't need things piling up my warehouse."

"It's not your warehouse. It's this company's, and I am the company. I am!"

"Deal with it. It is what it is," she said, using his phrase back on him. Fire with fire.

But he snapped back. "Oh no, that's not how it works. You don't get to say 'it is what it is.' Only I do. Only I get to say that, not you, not anyone else. Only I can take us to the next level. From this point forward you're done. I'm not going to let you ruin this company anymore than you've already done." Apparently, Tony thought he owned the phrase *it is what it is*.

"If you want to grow this company then get out there and sell and make profit on your jobs. Stop doing charity events that take away money I need to pay the bills!"

"I do my job," he shouted at the top of his voice. "I have grown this company to new heights. I have marketed it on social media and expanded its public relations to the community. I have spent countless hours networking with other businesses and growing our list of clients. I have created strategic partnerships. I have even stayed late to book deals with clients. I have put my time and energy into this company, building up its culture and creating a vision for our growth and this is how you repay me! You will fix what you have done, and you will do it now!"

"With what money? You took all of it for your stupid ass charity. I have nothing left, and none of your projects make any money, so what money am I supposed to have to buy your shit with? Get me sales and then we'll talk about expanding!"

"Paying the bills is not my problem. It's yours! I don't care if you have to take it out of your bank account. YOU WILL FIX THIS NOW!"

"How dare you! You will never have this company, ever. I will never let you have this company."

"Oh I will have it. I will, because dad sees what I'm doing and he likes it. So you better get with it, or I'll just have dad make you hand over your share."

"And maybe that might happen one day, but until then this is my company! MY WAY!"

"And what a great job you're doing,"

"You ungrateful piece of shit. Get out. Get out of my office! I don't want you in here anymore. All you're doing is holding us back. All you want to do is talk about growing and spend money; you don't even have a plan to expand you stupid ignoramus!"

"What are you talking about? I am the plan!"

Chapter 64

End of the Year Results

As the end of the year, the executive team met to review its progress. Of the entire sales team, Tony had the lowest profit margin, just shy of 8%. Everyone else was at least twenty percent. They started with Arthur. At once, Tom praised him. He had concluded the year with a series of exceptional bookings, including a $150,000 deal at 76% margin ($114,000), another at $54,000 at 74% ($39,960), and also a $68,000 deal at 79% ($53,720).

"I like the consistency," Tom said, giving him a spirited high-five. Victor was up next; he had contributed immensely to both his brother as well as the senior estimator. With Antonio, he had helped him earn $340,000 in contract work with an additional $371,000 dollars in service work.

"You've been busy," the coach joked.

"Hey, when you're the boss you gotta work."

Much of that success however had largely been due to Frank. When Victor and Barb had gone away to the spa, Tony had used the opportunity to suspend Frank; it not only hurt morale, but greatly affected production, as Frank was an indispensible foreman; without him, questions went unanswered, measurements were inaccurate, and the unforeseen cost the company dearly that his expertise would have otherwise prevented. Moreover, suspending Frank and putting Troy in charge of all the crews meant that Troy had no mentor and was thus forced into an unfair position of resolving issues he had neither the knowledge of nor the wherewithal to solve, a fact that deeply soured his friendship with Tony.

Then came Tony's numbers; he celebrated prematurely. Once again, he was counting leads. And again, Tom asked him what percentage he was taking credit for.

"All of them."

"All of them? So, you're taking credit for every else's numbers? Is that correct?"

He nodded.

"So, nobody in this room sold anything. Is that what you're trying to tell us? All of these numbers from

Arthur, your father, Antonio, and the senior estimator's are just extensions of your number. Is that what you're saying?"

"Yes."

"I'm going to say no to that," he replied.

"You can say no, but I'm taking credit for their numbers. I distributed the leads that became those sales, and so I'm taking credit for those leads."

"But you didn't actually sell the project did you? Did you! You're just taking credit for it even though they did all the work? I want to make sure I'm hearing you correctly?"

"I am the face of this company and I generate leads for the team."

"I thought Victor was the face of the company."

"We're in a transition phase?"

"We are?" he asked, suddenly turning to Barb and Victor for confirmation. Was this true? It wasn't. "And last I checked I thought last time we met we concluded- and Barb correct me if I'm wrong- that you were getting credit for distributing the leads, not for the actual sale.

"I get credit for distributing them and the sale."

He pulled out his calculator "Alright, let's put a number to what you're trying to say. Of your $400,000 in bookings you're claiming an additional $450,000 in leads, which is everyone else's numbers. Is this correct? Are you telling us you alone booked about a million dollars?"

He nodded.

"I'm not buying it. I'm not, because Victor is a hard worker. He's helped others with their numbers and Arthur has sold just as well as he did, and now you're telling me that what they sold should instead be credited to you. I call bullshit. I'm a professional, but I say that's bullshit!"

Chapter 65

Looking Ahead

The conversation quickly veered into talking about retirement as well as firing Antonio. "That is not your call," Victor said, rising from his chair in anger. The only person who could fire his brother was he, nobody else.

But Tony remained coldly defiant. "Then you need to own the decision and do something about him. We are a company moving forward and we cannot be slowed down by anything or anyone."

"Tony, drop it!"

"Dad, I'm glad to see you're taking an interest in the company as opposed to finding an excuse to leave, but we need to make changes if we are to grow, and that means getting rid of those that aren't profitable to the company."

"Speak for yourself, your numbers are shit."

"I do a lot more than sell. I promote this company on social media and through networking; I create leads and distribute them, and yes I do feel entitled to take credit for those, because I too have worked hard. But we can't grow if we continue on the same path as before."

"Then starting selling and stopping horsing around with stupid charities. We're a business after all. Arthur sells. I sell. My brother sells and so does my senior estimator. They all sell, except for you. Hell, even Arthur made me some cash going through the warehouse!"

It was true. Arthur's efforts had revamped the Operations Department creating a far more efficient and productive method of scheduling, warehouse storage, tools and fleet maintenance; of $175,000 worth of inventory metal, Arthur gave Victor $45,000 worth of recycled metal. That went right to the fleet and for buying new tools for the technicians; they couldn't thank Arthur enough.

Tony had resented that. "Every decision this company makes that involves numbers needs to go through me first. I should not be the last to hear about it."

"So what, I'm supposed to give you the forty-five grand so you can spend it on stupid furniture, or just pocket it? I don't think so. I'm the boss. I get the money."

"As the company's sales manager I have first dibs on it. The fact that Arthur excluded me goes against our core values of being a team player and promoting growth."

Tom looked puzzled. "How is that exactly? The money went to buy new tools for the crews and repair the trucks. How is that against promoting growth?"

"Because repairing trucks doesn't generate us any more revenue. Now, if we had used the money to buy another truck and hire another technician then we're using it to promote growth."

"So, technicians are to drive with defunct trucks?"

Tony shook his head. It dazzled him that someone he regarded so highly could be so dumb in matters of business. "Promoting growth is about what generates revenue, not what keeps us where we're at."

"I'm going to disagree," he replied. "Maybe I'm wrong here, but I would think a truck that works will get a technician to where he needs to be. Thus giving Sallie something to bill and thus earning the company money. If the truck doesn't even work then what's there to bill?"

Tony disagreed. A technician who wasn't where he needed to be was obviously not doing his job and thus not living up to the core values and therefore could in fact be fired.

Chapter 66

Family First

For over thirty years Antonio and Victor worked together. It wasn't perfect, but it was successful; they complimented their strengths and weaknesses, but what took three decades Tony ruined in less than five years.

* * * * * * * *

The coach was speechless. Tony's slanted view was utterly staggering; what world was he living in! It simply defied description. To assert Arthur had negated the core values by helping improve operations was utter lunacy, but Tony refused to see it any other way; and he wasn't done. He then went a step further and asserted that not only was everyone's leads his but that also they should be used to project ahead!

"I'm sorry, what," said Tom, still dazzled.

Tony wanted to claim the leads as actual numbers.

"That's preposterous. You can't do that."

"As a matter of fact I can," he said, going into another lecture as though he knew best; to Tony it made perfect sense. According to him, his answer was two-fold. First and foremost, his time was invaluable- more so than anyone else's- since he networked more than anyone else, spending mornings and evenings gaining evangelist fans to his ideas and building strategic partnerships as a result his time should therefore reflect growth. And secondly, since his leads hitherto had become sales that it only made sense that his leads should be a measure of forecasting ahead.

He then praised himself, congratulating this idea as both brilliant and promoting growth by further uniting his oversight with finance- if only his mother would open the books to him. Then they would truly be growing.

Tom politely listened. He had heard many crazy ideas throughout his career, but despite the lure and appeal they were nothing short of stunt tricks; they created awes and interest, but failed to substantiate. Claiming other's hard work was one thing, but to equate a lead to a booked sale was a recipe for catastrophe. Especially what he had been hearing about Joe's leads; after Amanda's dismissal,

Barb and Arthur had confided in him about the poor leads he was giving to Joe. Why on earth would she want to use cold leads to project ahead?

And that's exactly what Tom then asked Tony, who was quite suddenly taken aback in betrayal; how could his own mother go behind his back to discuss this matter with the coach; he was utterly horrified and disgusted; the fact that Arthur had also done so only picked at the injury more; his face reddened as he tried to remain calm.

"I am the sales manager and I pass leads to the sales team. If the sales agent does not follow up with my leads then that is not my fault. I disqualify leads and distribute them. That is my job and that is what I've been doing. I don't appreciate other members of this team going behind my back and discussing issues with our coach, because first of all that's not his job. We need to be a team that communicates, not one that goes behind other's backs. I work very hard here and I don't appreciate the negativity that's being thrown at me when I haven't done what I'm being accused of."

Barb wasn't impressed. She shot him down. "Don't play dumb with me. You've been giving Joe nothing but bad leads, because you've been spending all your time with that charity. Oh sure, they were probably good when you first got them, but then you run off and forget about them and by the time he gets them they're worthless."

"That's not true, mother. My charity fulfilled many purposes including help bring awareness to this company; we built many connections and I've been going to many new organizations and meetings as a result with the intent to generate new leads."

"But you drained us! You could have done that without us hosting a charity; you did your charity for your own ego, and now look at us. We can't pay our bills and I still have Joe getting overtime and HE'S NOT EVEN A TECHNICAN ANYMORE. I'm paying him ten hours of overtime a week to bring in sales from bad leads that you give him!"

But he just shook his head, as condescendingly as before. Neither Tom nor her nor apparently anyone at the table understood how to grow a business. "These are called opportunity costs. They are the costs to growing."

"Then do it on someone else's dime!"

"Mother, you're obviously having a difficult time with the idea of growing," he said pompously. "As the sales manager I distribute leads to the sales team; I network, generate leads and create reports to help the team see where we are and where we need to go. I am not responsible for underperforming agents, and I will certainly not apologize for moving Joe into sales. He's part of my expansion plan; he'll be running one of my branch offices, and I need him to understand how to sell; there's a learning curve, just like in everything.

"I filter all of our leads and distribute them. And it's up to the team to close the deal; I just distribute them. You're blaming me as if you got a bill in the mail and I'm the mailman. I'm just distributing. If you have a problem with Joe then we need to come together as a team, meet with him in private, and set some goals."

"That's your job," she said. "That's what you should have already done with him."

"I didn't realize until this moment that he was struggling this badly. I know his numbers are done, but then so is every new agent's numbers. It's a learning curve."

He refused to lose his temper. Despite his feelings of indignation towards her he remained calm and collected, which only served to exasperate her more; as the two went back and forth she got louder and more belligerent, calling him out for single-handedly ruining the company. He of course objected, instead praising his efforts. Finally, Tom intervened.

"What about the rest of the team generating leads? I have to believe that a technician is rewarded for getting a referral; their word goes a long way."

He nodded. "The crews are encouraged to get referrals and leads, but the sales team lets me do that."

He again looked puzzled. "So, you're saying that nobody in the sales team but you generates leads, but doesn't Victor and Arthur network also?"

It was true. They both did and also generated leads, which had been the epicenter of much debate. Tony wanted all leads to go through him, but then did that mean his dad and his would be brother-in-law had to turn theirs over to him? According to Tony, that's exactly what they had to do. Then Tony would sort through them, select the ones he liked, and distribute the ones he didn't. He fervently denied keeping any for himself, but the evidence against him was too strong.

Now it was Victor and Arthur's turn to speak up in the meeting and the seismic waves they created nearly ruffled Tony's rage; he laboriously tried to stay composed, but it was clear his face was about to explode. While Victor was at first proud of his son's efforts with the charity event he was dismayed at his negligence to follow up on a list of 150 strong leads that were in need of restoration; of an average $15,000 a piece this equated to a potential $2.2m in revenue for the company; easy fruit at the bottom of the tree and yet somehow Tony had ignored the list, allowing the competition to sweep it up. The fact that several of those were already clients of the company only further disappointed Victor, who had given his word to them.

But Tony just shook his head, innocent of any charges. "Those were not filtered leads, dad. They were not good leads."

"But I gave them my word. The least you can do is go there and take a look."

"It's a waste of my time. My time is better served networking and disqualifying leads; as I've said before, let me handle the lead generation."

"But they've been a client of ours for ten years!"

"That may be so, but my time is precious. I'm too important of an asset to this company to go running around, even for clients of ours."

Victor started to get loud. "It's seven times harder to get a new client than to keep an existing one."

"I couldn't agree more. In fact, that's what I keep telling you," Tony said. "But they like us and they continue to give us business; just because we don't follow up with one issue of theirs isn't the end of the world."

"Of course it is! I'm the boss. If I say go then you go. You got it!"

"Dad, there's no need to get loud. We're all talking like professionals here."

"I can fire you if I want to."

"You absolutely can. That is your right, but just know that I've been doing everything I can to help grow this company."

But if he meant to sound remorseful he failed; in everything there was a tone of condescending, and neither Barb nor Victor knew where it came from. For every hardship they had endured it seemed incomparable to the contentions they faced with Tony; where did he learn to be such a pompous ass? He flagrantly ignored the rules, disobeyed their directions and did things his way; where was the humility, the willingness to study and learn and make mistakes? Sallie showed it, even Arthur, but with Tony he apparently had all the answers.

Decades had been spent in struggle, trying to put food on the table and for what, a snobbish brat of a child? They had made incredible sacrifices from working out of a tiny closet to being on the verge of bankruptcy, and still they endured, but not for themselves, but for their children. And now they were asking themselves why.

Victor was physically worn. His skin was callused, his hair gray, and his nails diseased; his eyes strained and his hearing was bad; how many cold night had he worked with nothing but a single incandescent light bulb to illuminate his workspace. But he never complained. He did it all for his children; he kept his chin up, bit the icy wind and worked until his hands were frozen. If he had hoped his sacrifices had engrained any sense of work ethic into Tony he was sadly mistaken; the boy never understood.

"All I've tried to do dad, is help you become an owner, but you insist on being a technician. You're not. Those days are over; you don't have to be that anymore. That's what we have the crews for."

"I TREAT THEM LIKE HOW I WANT TO BE TREATED. They are not slaves!"

"Nobody says they're slaves. If they want to work someplace else they can. It's a free country."

"But you exhaust them! You treat our technicians like they were yours to do as you please and you've never done a hard day's work in your life."

"That's because I have a bad shoulder," he said, as if that excused it; he didn't even help his aged uncle unload truck deliveries. He made him do it entirely.

"You're a spoiled brat is what you are."

"I'm sorry you see it that way."

At that Tom once again interjected. Perhaps it was time to revaluate the core values. "I'm seeing a lot of tension here still, and the definitions of certain values seem to be disagreeable. Is there any value in particular that has caused the most disagreement?"

Sallie spoke up. "Spirited. I hate it."

"How does everyone else feel about it?" Only Tony wanted to keep it; Arthur meanwhile shied away, trying to hide his thoughts. Tom called on him. "Arthur?"

He hesitated to speak. Something had been on his mind the entire time, but he didn't know how to say it.

"It's okay. Say what you got to say."

He took a deep breath, still feeling unsure. Ever since Tony had called him up wanting his support to fire his family he had felt uneasy, especially during the charity event; it felt very hypocritical then. He looked at everyone: Before him there had been nothing. There had been no executive team, almost no communication, poor leadership, mismanaged departments, poor sales and no ability to forecast ahead, and utterly deplorable morale. Because of his industrial efforts all of that had changed.

His strategies had revived the company; they now hired on the basis of his three principles: can the candidate meet the company's objectives; does the candidate possess the necessary competencies to fulfill his or her duties; and can the candidate adapt to an every-changing climate? He was an advocate of empowering others, and believed that leadership was all about inspiring new leaders. Whereas Tony believed leadership as an exclusive club he invited all in; with Arthur, there were no grandiosity. He was not one for speeches. He took the lead, climbed the precipice first and faced any dangers head-on with persistence and stanch perseverance.

He had become Barb's key advisor. Under his guidance, she made critical financial decisions that ensured the stability of the company; he negotiated with the bank and other CFOs when the company was in dire straits, helping it navigate to safer waters. When she confided the need to fire employees he accepted the burden and sold until everyone's job was secure; he sold and he sold high. He saved the company money where it could and earned higher and higher profits.

He earned respect, not because he felt entitled to it, but because he earned it. He started at 4 AM and he finished at 11 PM and he worked on the weekends too; and he was only paid for forty hours. He straddled to grow the company and Tony's personality, and every day it seemed that clash only exacerbated; the two never saw eye-to-eye. And the fact that he had asked him to expel his family but then hosted a charity for the benefit of others seemed as contradictory as anything.

And so, taking a deep, he felt the team should know who Tony really was. He rejected the core value of Spirited by denouncing Tony; if Tony really wanted to keep the core value then he would have to explain to the team why he so flagrantly disobeyed it. Would he really try and argue how firing his family was being spirited? Knowing Tony, he would.

The room fell silent. Everyone was aghast. Tom dropped his jaw. Unbelievable. For someone who preached being spirited by hosting a charity the fact that he had actually tried to fire his family stood as testimony to the invalidity of the core value and why it should be removed.

Up until now, Tony had channeled his rage. All at once his face flushed with anger and he couldn't control it any longer; his hand smacked the table hard and as though he was leaping across the table he pointed straight at Arthur. "THIS IS MY FAMILY AND I WILL SAY AND DO WHATEVER I WANT TO THEM, BECAUSE THEY ARE MY FAMILY. NOT YOURS! WHEN- NOT IF- BUT WHEN I BECOME CEO YOU WILL DO AS I

SAY AND OBEY EVERY DECISION I MAKE, AND YOU WILL KEEP YOUR GODDAMN MOUTH SHUT!

"I LOVE MY FAMILY VERY MUCH, AND I WILL DO WHATEVER IT TAKES TO PROTECT THEM AND HELPS THEM GROW STRONGER, SO HOW DARE YOU INSINUATE THAT I DON'T LOVE THEM. HOW DARE YOU! EVERYTHING I DO IS FOR THEM. EVERYTHING!" He raised his voice so loud that the people outside the room became frightened and someone wondered if the police should be called.

"I AM THE VISIONARY OF THIS COMPANY AND I KNOW BEST. I HAVE MADE COUNTLESS SACRIFICIES, AND I AM LEADING THE CHANGE HERE, NOT YOU. I AM TAKING THIS COMPANY TO NEW HEIGHTS, BUT ALL YOU EVERY DO IS PIGGYBACK OFF OF MY SUCCESS.

"YOU ARE A LEECH, A DISEASE, AND I AM THE CURE. YOU ARE A SNAKE TRYING TO GET INTO MY HOUSE AND I WON'T LET YOU. DO YOU HEAR ME? I WILL NOT LET YOU COME BETWEEN MY FAMILY AND ME!"

Chapter 67

The Queen

As the meeting ended, Tony caught Arthur at the door. He buried his finger into his chest, "If you want to be rich and successful, then you'll do exactly as I say," he said in a sharp half whisper. "And when I'm CEO, you will not be on this team!"

* * * * * * * *

If not for Sallie begging he would have left, but she did and so he stayed; despite all his efforts to help her Tony did everything to bring her down. He continued to attack her self-esteem, ridiculing her lifestyle as settling and uneventful; he badgered her to lose weight, dress more expensively, and harassed her to enroll in higher education; she failed the LSAT three times, but not without Arthur trying to help her; Tony's idea of helping was to belittle, or what he called pushing her untapped potential. When law school was out of the question he pushed her into public speaking; by pushing he volunteered her.

As time went on, she became less of her old self, and more of his puppet; less happy with life, she yielded to him and surrendered who she was to become something she wasn't; when she couldn't afford the clothing and jewelry because he refused to give her a raise she had no choice but to turn to Arthur; he gave himself the raise instead. Arthur did his best to console her, but he refused to empty his pockets; the more Tony pushed her the more she and Arthur fought.

Their quarrels led to distance, but each time she came back to him, apologizing and crying; she felt helpless against Tony's domineering personality. She confided this into Arthur, hugging him tightly and pouring out her heart; she wanted to tell her brother off, but it always ended in him winning. She felt like a victim and she couldn't escape.

And as she battled between a tug-of-war of being true to herself and what her brother wanted her to be she felt like Arthur was slipping away; many nights she cried in her sleep. She had lost so much weight, but Tony continued to call her fat; despite her athletic physique she had lost all passion and intimacy faded from the relationship. In the meanwhile, Tony boasted publicly about his, how much fellatio he was getting, and how his relationship was getting serious; he got upset when Sallie didn't share his happiness.

And as he brought her down further so he felt better about himself. So good in fact that he spent $3,500 on multiple trade shows that earned the company no leads; he went on more vacation-business trips; and blasted social media with videos of the company as a great place to work. As with everything, he deferred to the core values.

He claimed he upheld the core values more than anyone else, but left Arthur at a trade show for six hours. "I start things only. It's up to others to see them through." This is how he defined Promoting Growth; his Work Ethic was about starting, never finishing. He also defined it as staying home and calling clients in his pajamas. When Arthur challenged him and his definitions he threatened to fire him on account of violating the core value of Team Player. "I do what I want to do, because I can, but you have to do what I say, or else."

Nearly everyday they clashed, and every time Barb backed Arthur up. She gave him her full support. When Tony compared the company to his relationship with his partner he said, "Just like how my partner sets the rules at our house and I follow them, so I expect you will do the same for me." Arthur disagreed. He followed Barb's rules.

"Being a team player means helping others."

Tony shook his head. He disagreed. "No, it's about who has the better ideas, and you don't. Everything you have done is because of me. Just like with my partner and I. He listens because I have all the good ideas."

As the weeks passed and Tony's dialogue became more about marriage so his mother attacked him for his slanted views on the subject; she related everything back to the office and how to conduct business rather than attack his homosexuality. "Marriage is about equal partnerships," she said. "Just like your father and me. We equally share a part in the business."

"Mom, you don't ever talk to dad," he replied harshly. "Before I came around nobody even knew you existed at the company." She slammed the door in his face. Offended, she refused to talk to him for a week. But she wasn't alone in hating him: even his future mother-in-law refused to talk to him.

A businesswoman herself, Tony's future mother-in-law resented how he spoke to her son; his overbearing sense of self-importance was loathsome. Moreover, she feared for her son's financial future if Tony was in fact going to inherit the company; the way it sounded it was headed straight into the ground. Interestingly enough, Barb shared her repugnance and happily wished to remain her friend if the relationship fell apart; when the two lovebirds announced they were buying a home together the two mothers both expressed concern:

As suspected, Tony dominated the decision-making process. He picked out a townhouse and settled on renting out the two first floors; while his partner was still looking over the condition of the premises he was miles ahead, advertising the rental space and buying furniture before the paperwork had even been signed; ignoring the details he was light-years ahead.

And so his future mother-in-law intervened. She refused to let his name be on the loan; the fact that neither Tony nor his partner could even afford the place didn't stop him from wanting it. And so, she bought it. Tony was delighted, even though she only gave him 10% stake in the property. The rest went to her, and in her absence her son; she cut Tony out of all financial decisions. But that didn't stop him from persuading his partner to continue with the plan to rent out the floors. Now Tony was a landlord and with no financial responsibility; it was a dream come true.

Chapter 68

The Phone Call

Unlike Tony, his partner was athletically built, docile and introverted. In private, he admitted to Arthur that the rules in their home were actually Tony's. He said Tony gave him a list and he got to pick from it.

* * * * * * * *

One day, Arthur received an unexpected phone call telling him that his mother was in the hospital. At once, he took the first flight home. While waiting nervously in the waiting room his phone rang. It was Sallie. Excitedly, he answered it. Unfortunately, she didn't call to reassure him. She called to break up with him.

Chapter 69

The Heart that Doesn't Beat

Arthur collapsed against the chair; the phone slipped from his hand. Of all the times and places, and she had broken up with him now. For the next hour he just stared blankly at the wall in front of him.

He had begun his career wishing to be a teacher, but he neither had the network nor the opportunity to become one and so he had gone into sales. There he had met Sallie and felt this might be his life. Now his world was crashing. For what seemed the longest hour of his life, he sat in that waiting room wondering how it had come to this.

That night he called Tom to thank him for everything. The coach surprised him with his own news.

"Actually, I should be the one thanking you," he said. "I'll admit I had my suspicions that something like this might happen; obviously, I didn't wish for it to happen to you, and I'm sorry it did. But I've been giving it a lot of thought and I'm probably not going to renew my contract with the company. Just between you and me, the writing is on the wall."

Chapter 70

Doing What Must be Done

When Barb learned the news she just stared at her laptop. How could Sallie do such a thing? Arthur was perfect for her. He was loyal, caring, devoted, hard working, and had showed her endless love; he was everything she wanted in a son-in-law. Too stunned to do any work she left the office early. How had it come to this?

Arthur had been a pleasure. She had enjoyed his company, his humor, and his willingness to learn new things. She admired how others respected him, and how receptive he was to new ideas; he never pushed her to do anything, but instead suggested advice to her. She had loved his enthusiasm, and appreciated his eagerness to accompany her to church, buying groceries, or even help her prepare dinner; when they had talked the conversation was never about business, but on things she liked such as spiritualism.

He was accountable, responsible, and intelligent, and she had come to rely upon his advice in nearly every financial decision of the company; although she had final say she often deferred to him; he exercised more power than anyone at the company, but his modesty always put others first; selfless, his decisions were made in the welfare of the company rather than himself, and he owned his decisions, right or wrong.

When he was tasked with restructuring several departments he did so in less than thirty days, cross-training technicians and staff; under his leadership, nobody was laid off, but rather instead morale soared, sales boomed, and profit margins were never higher; before him the company averaged 30% profit margin. Under him, that number soared to fifty-five percent. And by cross-training he glossed a return of $600,000 to a department that had once been losing $200,000 a year.

He was a man of his word. He listened, took notes, and worked hard to earn other's respect. Barb simply couldn't thank him enough. He had given her company new life, and though she had only paid him forty hours a week he easily earned three times that much; he was worth every penny and more. And now, for the first time in a long time she cried.

A. Ruben

The Final Six Months

Chapter 71

No Promises

Tony's partner shared with Arthur how difficult it was being a landlord. Apparently, Tony wasn't doing anything but collecting the rent; he refused to handle any of the problems since his name wasn't on the mortgage. He claimed that collecting was fulfilling his 10% stake.

* * * * * * * *

Arthur had no reason to stay, but as he started to pack his bags and clean out his desk Barb stopped him; she begged him to stay. "I should have had a son like you," she said, apologizing for everything. "I cannot tell you how much I am indebted to you for everything you have done." She asked him to remain on the executive leadership team.

She praised him and thanked him, especially for dating her daughter, admitting how happy she was seeing him with her; she had seen how much her daughter had matured with him. Despite her capitulation, Sallie had become a strong, independent woman. "You will always have my thanks," she said, offering him a hopeful smile.

"There's nothing left for me here."

"I can't make you stay, but I think you should know how much she cries nowadays. I see her hide her face as she goes into the bathroom. She still cares about you."

"Then why did she do it?"

She sighed heavily. "You know why."

"And yet, he's still here. He will always be here. Unless you do something he will run this company and you've told me enough times what will happen. I've tried, Barb. I've tried, but it looks like even I can't win. He's taken everything from me."

"Stay."

"For what reason?"

"For her."

"She broke up with me, Barb! I'm sorry, but what do you want me to say. I've given this place everything, but unless you do something I can't give you what you asked.

Do you remember what that was? You wanted this place to grow, and I believe I've done that for you."

She understood his frustration. "You have kept your word. I know that."

"But unless you do something about Tony it won't last, and you know it," he said regretfully.

"I need you. Please, Arthur. Stay."

He stopped what he was doing. "Why Barb?" But she had nothing to offer him, not even a place in the succession plan; the writing was on the wall. It was only a matter of time before Tony took over and fired him.

Chapter 72

Hospital Visits

She had nothing to offer him, and he had every reason to leave but against his better judgment he stayed; he needed the extra money anyway for moving expenses; at 29 years old he was an executive. He had grown a company to new heights, earned a name in the market, and had the respect of the company; whereas he had struggled to secure work before now he was highly desired; at networking events, CEOs and presidents alike chased after him. If there was any reason to stay it was for repaying Barb for taking the risk in hiring him.

Barb was eternally grateful. Without him she felt like she was losing an ally, and she needed as many allies as possible in her battle against Tony; only with Arthur did she feel strong enough to put her foot down. Reinvigorated, she now canceled the leases he had forced to sign again; she disposed of the second group of furniture, and mandated that no bid or quote was to be less than 20% margin. She then took a step even further and required Tony to submit a weekly sales report to her. If she meant to provoke a storm she got one.

Tony flew into a rage. All at once, he protested her intrusion into what he felt was his authority. Not only did he force her to renew the contracts and retrieve the furniture in person, and demanded direct access into the accounting system (she had changed her password and refused to give it to him.) He rejected her mandate, telling her he would continue to meet competitor's pricing and give away projects for free as he saw fit.

Because he forced her to pull the furniture out of the dumpster she pulled out her back; he had refused to let anyone help her or even give her any tools to use such as the forklift. He made her do it by hand in the hot sun; he even called a companywide meeting to have every employee watch her do it: this was her punishment for violating the core values of Promoting Growth and being Resourceful.

He then badgered her to retire while she was lying on her bed. The following day she went to the hospital.

Chapter 73

Confidential Reviews

Taking her doctor's advice, Barb got some rest. She also enrolled in yoga classes and began walking more; every night she had a glass or two or three of wine.

* * * * * * * *

As the executive leadership team sat down at the next monthly meeting, Tony unexpectedly ambushed his mother. He announced he had just completed annual performance reviews- a right he asserted was his since he administrated HR- and felt it necessary to share some of the feedback. Apparently, many if not all employees felt that Barb was doing a poor job as CEO; the comments were so negative it was daunting to believe they were real.

Negative, vulgar, even the point of degrading the comments were excessively offensive; Barb was taken aback as was everyone else. How could anyone write something so insulting, and of all people Antonio and the senior estimator? A few read: *This company is sinking because of her. Things were better before she started running the show. Who died and made her God?* Tom was flabbergasted. Never had he ever heard such direct attacks against an owner.

"The truth is sometimes hard to hear," said Tony, regretfully. "But when a leader is inefficient it is the responsibility of others to step up and do what is necessary to steer a new course; the proof is in the pudding, mom. I know you don't want to hear it from me, which is why I felt it important to let you hear it from others. These are your employees; these are their words.

"I know we haven't agreed in the past, but part of my job is to do performance reviews and this was the feedback. I'm sorry if it hurts, but this is what people are saying about your leadership. I know you don't want to hear it but maybe it's time for you to retire and allow Sallie and I to take over.

"Sallie has been improving herself. Look at how much weight she's lost. She's really taken the initiative and I couldn't be more proud of her. I can see she really cares about herself and about improving this company. Together we can make you and dad proud. I know it's hard to hear, but retirement is an option; you and dad deserve it. You have worked so hard and given Sallie and I such a great opportunity."

She crossed her arms defiantly. "And what Antonio," she asked, still unsure of what to make of his negative remarks. "Are you going to fire him or anyone else that spoke badly about me?"

"If that's what you want, but we really can't allow this kind of negativity to exist. It not only holds us back, but it also creates a very toxic climate, and we are a great place to work."

"So you would fire him?"

"If that's what you and dad wanted. We are about promoting growth. These comments are not that."

Barb refused to retire. She had her suspicions and within twenty-four the truth came to light. Tony had in fact manipulated the reviews: he had inserted loaded questions that left employees with no option but to be critical. It had backed every employee into a corner, because Tony had threatened to fire each one if they didn't answer.

Antonio publicly condemned Tony as unethical, immoral, and highly unprofessional. "I don't know him anymore," he said resentfully to Barb. "That's not the boy I watched grow up."

Chapter 74

Disillusioned

One stormy afternoon, Tony received a frantic phone call from his partner telling him that their basement had just flooded. At once, Tony rushed over to supervise his partner clean up the water; he told him to ignore the water in the walls though. When the tenant complained of mildew Tony just raised his rent higher.

* * * * * * * *

In the meanwhile, Troy had become disillusioned; his friendship with Tony strained with each decision of his. His friend's insensitivity towards others, arrogance, and utterly dumb decisions had exasperated his ability to work at the company; whenever he had an idea Tony dismissed it.

And when Frank had been inexplicably suspended from the company the stress mounted. All at once, project managers barraged him for answers that he didn't have; he tried his best, but Victor was away with Barb and so he had nobody to turn to. The crews did their best, but there were just some issues that were just too big, and though he tried his best his inexperience jeopardized the company's reputation as well as its budgets. But was he to blame? After all, he had just wanted to be a technician. It had been Tony that had put him in charge.

The crews didn't blame him, but Tony did. As the problems piled up so did the number of disgruntled clients and losses to budgets; several clients even pulled their contracts. As deadlines passed he got heat from all ends and despite doing his best he simply had to admit his lack of expertise and experience were the root.

But to add insult to injury, he resented Tony's decision to move Joe into sales. He needed every technician and argued to no avail; Tony would not budge. He refused to retract his decision, insisting that he was merely helping Troy discover his untapped potential. "Sometimes we have to work with less in order to discover what we're really made of."

But the final straw was the emergency calls. His crews had no time to rest, no family time, no spousal time; many were working twenty hours a day. The crews were utterly exhausted; mistakes followed, and profits vanished. But the one person who could fix it refused; Tony would not change his mind. He was a self-proclaimed visionary and insisted his ideas were golden.

Troy ultimately turned to Arthur. It seemed if anyone could resolve problems it was he. "I don't know what to do. I'm so overwhelmed; there are problems with every job and he doesn't listen anymore. Hell, I don't even know him anymore. I thought I knew Tony, but that's not the Tony I knew. Whoever that is has lost his mind!"

Arthur listened as he vented. "All I really want to do is work on trucks. That's really what I'm good at, and these trucks need a good look-at. But instead I'm out there trying to solve problems that I don't have the answers to, and I'm pretty sure he intends to replace Frank with me."

Arthur had had his suspicions. Everyone had. "But if he thinks I'm going to replace him then he's nuts. I'm not Frank. I'm not Victor. I'm just someone who'd rather be working on trucks. Meanwhile he's wherever the hell he is doing whatever the hell he does walking on clouds and coming up with the most stupidest ideas ever."

Chapter 75

The Mentor

Troy was ready to quit. All because of Tony.

* * * * * * * *

Frank was beloved by the technicians. He was respectful, loyal, reliable, and accountable, but there was little he could do to help Troy. They had spoken on the phone while he was suspended, but without actually being on-site there was little he could do; for the sake of the company he tried to help.

He had taken the young man under his wing, guided his learning, and had begun to show him what to look for when Tony abruptly suspended him. Until that moment however he mentored Troy from start to finish.

"Look, listen and learn," he had said. "And never argue with the customer. It's not that he or she is right. It's just that they don't know. It's their job to ask questions and it's your job to have the answers, so be patient and teach."

On a number of occasions, Troy got to see that in action. A frustrated client insisted that Frank was wrong, but no matter how long or how loud he shouted Frank had remained calm. Then he spoke and softly explained the technicalities behind the problem; once the client realized he knew what he was talking about he shifted gears and listened attentively; he humbly apologized and from that point on went straight to Frank whenever an issue arose.

"Remember," Frank told Troy. "It's your word against his. So you better know what you're talking about."

Another time a project manager erred and tried to pass the blame onto Frank, but the superintendent proved him wrong. Instead of shifting the blame however, which he easily could have done, he instead let it drop. "People respect you when you can solve their problems. So don't point the finger. Instead, be glad someone is pointing at you. This way you can get all credit when you're right."

Chapter 76

At the Table

Frank had refused to tear up his hopes and dreams the time Tony had forced everyone to submit to his vision. He was a grandfather and nothing or nobody was going to tell him that his grandson's future was second best.

* * * * * * * *

Despite all efforts, Tony continued to try and fire Frank as well as his uncle but to no avail; neither Barb nor Victor would have it. Even when he brought candidates to replace them they refused. "I hired them when I first started this company," said Victor forcefully, "and until I draw my last breath both of them will have a job here!"

"Dad, part of growing is leaving the past behind."

"I am the owner of this company! Whatever I say goes and that's final!"

"Then I'll just have to decide when you retire."

"And where does it say I'm leaving the company to you? I could leave it with your sister or Arthur, or I could just sell it and you'll have to find a new job if the owner doesn't want to keep you."

"Really dad. Who's going to buy this company? I'm the only asset that has any value here, so nobody is going to buy the company, because I'm too integral. Besides, Sallie can barely do her job; she's crying so much- it's all I see her doing. She runs into the bathroom and cries for hours. Why is she crying? I'll tell you why, because you and mom are making life very difficult for her. That's why. She want's to grow this place just like me, but you're not letting her discover her untapped potential."

"Screw you asshole," shouted Sallie. She was just coming out of the bathroom and had heard him. "You don't know shit about me. So why don't you mind your own fucking business!"

"And there's another reason why she can't run things. She's too emotional all the time."

She flicked him off as she went back to her desk.

"What this company needs is drive, and I've been doing my best, dad, but you and mom have got to let it go. It's time to retire and allow me the opportunity to take this company where it needs to go."

"Then I'm leaving it all to Arthur. He knows how to sell and I've never heard anyone say anything bad about him. All I hear day in and day out around here is how much he's helping my company grow. He got me money from recycling stuff in our warehouse and new tools for the technicians and that's a winner in my book."

"Dad," he said, trying to minimize Arthur's efforts. "He's only done these things, because I told him to do it. You're thanking him when the credit really goes to me. Every success of this company came from me."

"Then why did he do it and not you? Why are my crews looking to him for answers? Why aren't they coming to you? Explain that to me?"

"Because that's called designating authority. It's what leaders do. They're thanking him, because I told him what to do and he's a good follower. He takes directions well and obeys like a good employee."

He doubted that. "So you're saying if I left him the company that Arthur would run it into the ground?"

"Yes, that's what I'm saying. I mean look at his relationship with Sallie. They're not even together anymore. If he can't even hold a relationship together then how do you expect him to hold a company together?"

"And yet, he's still here. Isn't he? He could have left; what reason does he have to stay if he and Sallie aren't together anymore? You tell me! Any of my employees can leave anytime they wish, but he's stays and why? Maybe it's because he actually knows how to do his job! Maybe it's because instead of trying to grab this company he's out there selling and making me money. That's the kind of leader I like to see. He sells. He gets respect around here, and from what I hear he's been a big help to Antonio and the senior estimator as well as your mother. So, why shouldn't he lead this company? Why should I leave everything to him?"

Tony became anxious; he was treading troubled waters. The only person who deserved the company was he, not Sallie or Arthur. "He and Sallie broke up. That means he really can't be trusted. He shouldn't be coming over to the house anymore. He shouldn't be in mom's office, or even on the executive team. He can't be trusted. This is a family business and we can't afford to have anyone jeopardize that. He knows too much; he needs to go."

"He is still family."

"Are you serious? She broke up with him. That means he shouldn't even be working here. He knows too much of what goes on behind this operation and he could easily go out and give it our competition. He's not as loyal as you think. He's selfish and manipulative. He's only out for his own gain now."

Victor got loud. "So that's why he's out there selling now is it? That's why his numbers I hear are greater than yours, because he's trying to sabotage this company? I would give him permission to tell my competition everything about this company if it meant keeping him, because I trust him. Whatever reason he has for not dating Sallie is between the two of them; it's not my business and it's not yours. So, stop trying to take this company from your mother and me and go out and sell!

"He leaves whenever he wishes. And he's staying on the executive team, because that's what I want and so does your mother. He's been honest to Sallie this whole time; she's never said a word of him cheating on her. So whatever their reason is it isn't honesty, which means I will trust him and that's the end of it!"

Tony jumped into a crazy dance. "That's insane! He's not part of this family anymore, and if aren't willing to fire him then I will, but I won't risk you jeopardizing my inheritance. If you won't fire him then I will!"

"TONY, THIS IS MY BUILDING AND MY RULES, AND I'LL DO AS I PLEASE. IF I SAY HE STAYS THEN HE STAYS. GOT IT!"

"And that's why you and mom are holding us back. You can't let go of the past."

Chapter 77

The Senior Estimator

For six months, Sallie gave Arthur the cold shoulder, but it wasn't that she hated him. It's that she was too ashamed and couldn't bring herself to tell him the truth. Tony had made her do it.

* * * * * * * *

As long as Tony brought in revenue there was little Barb could do to silence his evangelistic spread of his vision; every day he boasted how great he was and how his vision was inspiring change; he claimed other's success as his own, using it as proof of his genius and rightful claim as heir. Although those in the company knew better others outside on the periphery adored him and his charisma.

Though Barb and Victor innately loved their son they despised his personality; his ego was so high it had air rights over skyscrapers. And when he began having the senior estimator and Antonio write his quotes for him he discovered just how much more time he had to devote to his charity foundation; the two were already swamped and this only added to their burden.

In addition to his own quotes the senior estimator was already exhausted from following up on the quotes of purged agents; every agent had had dozens in the pipe when Tony abruptly pointed his finger at them like a gunslinger. Now it was up to the senior estimator to sort it out; he divided it among his team, but it still proved overbearing- and if it sold then he spent additional time interacting with the project management team. But if that wasn't enough he also followed up on any leads Victor gave him.

Exhausted, he eventually gave up his weekends to come into the office. He slept during his lunch and ate breakfast at his desk; he was as fatigued as the crews, and Tony dumped quote after quote on him, expecting it to be done within twenty-four hours, an impossible task when too often he had to reach out to suppliers for costing; he stayed late at the office and arrived early and soon brought in a pillow to catch a quick catnap at his desk.

Tony however used this as an excuse to try and fire him. "We are a company moving forwards and cannot afford to have people around that simply can't keep up."

But the senior estimator was too tired to protest. Of eight former agents, he had to follow up, reply, answer questions, change pricing as needed, try a different contact if the person on the other end was no longer the decider, and keep record of his activity; if awarded the contract he had to review the details with the project management team, which could easily consume half of his day; of an average 35 quotes per purged agent, about 280 possible contracts, this amounted to a potential four million dollars.

And the fact that Tony now wanted him to quote for him meant he had to prioritize Tony ahead of everyone else; after repeatedly reprimanded for getting quotes late to clients he made this his first task of the day. Consequently, this meant nobody could bother him until after lunch, because Tony dumped boxes upon boxes of clients on him; on any given day, he had about forty quotes to do for Tony.

To add insult to injury, Tony, who felt he knew his client best, often reversed any instruction the senior estimator gave to the project management team; in minutes he undid hours of review. And if the project lost money the blame somehow fell on him, because as Tony often said,

"I'm not Operations." He claimed his job was just to shake hands and go get the next contract.

Chapter 78

Push and Pull

Like the senior estimator, Antonio also became fatigued. When he refused to stay late to handle emergency calls Tony tried to use the core values to fire him. "But I'm your uncle," he protested. Tony just shook his head.

"You're still an employee."

* * * * * * * *

In addition to advocating for their termination Tony also dismissed any responsibility. As the sales manager and someone who claimed all numbers had to go through him first it amazed others how he could blame Antonio and the senior estimator when he was technically their manager. Where was his accountability?

295

But according to Tony, he had tried to help them discover their untapped potential, a phrase he loved to use, but if they failed it was only because of their own doing, not his; he took no responsibility for the actions of others, unless of course they succeeded. "A manager doesn't manage, but rather seeks to improve others and one of our core values is about promoting growth. So, if someone fails to meet our higher standards than it's time to reconsider their employment with us."

And yet, while he delegated tasks he spent more time with his charity and getting buy-in for his vision; he enrolled five employees into a motivational program of his favorite speaker at a cost of $1,200 per person; and because he got so revved up he treated himself to another program at a higher cost of $8,000. "We cannot move forward until we feel like we are already there."

He then spent an additional $6,000 on sales training that was neither beneficial nor in line with how the company did business; bored, Tony walked out of seminar, but expected everyone else to stay; for whatever reason he then spent an additional $2,000 afterwards on sales tools from that firm; everything went right on a shelf to collect dust. But much to Sallie's dismay, he wasn't done spending.

Filled with the allure of being a landlord he tried to rent out part of the warehouse. He asked for $5,500 a month, but ignored the repairs needed; the fact that there was no restroom was inconsequential not to mention the part of the warehouse he wanted to rent out had no truck door for loading/unloading; Tony put all repairs on the would-be renter, and surprisingly he had many offers. It never happened though, owing much to Barb and Arthur, who refused to take on the liability.

And Sallie too set his plans back. She had had it with Joe being in sales. "For the love of God, just let him be a technician! I have nothing to bill his overtime to." At closer analysis, Joe was the fourth highest paid employee at the company; in order, Barb, Victor and Tony made more. At almost $69,000, Joe also surpassed every technician by at least ten thousand dollars. He even made more than Frank and Antonio. But his price tag was owed entirely to Tony, and for that Sallie erupted at him; in his last six months at the company, Arthur never heard a more belligerent fight in his life than that one between Sallie and her brother.

Chapter 79

Pushing Back

When Tony still refused to budge on him Barb cut off his company credit card. She also removed his eligibility from any bonuses; until he moved Joe back as a technician she would cut him off at the knees. She then required, but knew better, that all sales agents report their appointments for the day. Not surprisingly, Tony refused.

In swift retaliation, she refused to reimburse any receipts over 30 days. For anyone else this was no problem. But Tony often held onto his for as long as six months, dumping them on his mother and sister and expecting a quick turnaround. Moreover, Barb instituted a new policy that any expenditure had to be first approved by her otherwise it would not be reimbursed. Again, Tony refused to comply.

Barb then hired a Human Resources Manager to replace Tony; despite being forced to agree to it before she never truly recognized Tony's overseer of the department. And with the new manager, she placed HR under the direction supervision of the Finance Department, pushing Tony out of the picture. Unfortunately, Tony accused her of violating the core values on her third day and fired her while his mother was out to lunch; Barb tried to call her back but the woman decided against it. As such, Tony resumed his role as head of HR.

Barb then tried to hire another estimator, but again her efforts were stymied. Tony insisted she was intruding into his area of supervision and refused to allow the senior estimator to participate in the interview; he further threatened to fire whoever his mother hired the second he or she stepped foot inside the building. "Legally, I can fire anyone just for breathing," he said.

Chapter 80

Hardball

At the next executive meeting the topic of Joe resurfaced. It had been tabled on a number of occasions since the company had begun meeting with Tom, and every time the debate met an impasse; despite being heavily outnumbered, even by the coach, Tony refused to budge.

"Let me remind the group that oxygen is the most important thing a company can have," he said, hoping to change the results. "If we don't have cash then we don't have a company, and if technicians are our best way of generating cash quickly then we need to be exploring that option with more attention. Without cash, we can't grow."

But while Tony agreed he wasn't ready to sacrifice his vision. "Cash is king, but growth requires vision."

"But without cash we can't do anything."

"Part of us growing as a team is recognizing the value of ideas, and when we begin to implement the ideas that I have we will begin to grow faster than we've ever thought possible." Barb tried to interrupt but Tony kept going. "I'm all for increasing our number of technicians, but we can't just think about our one location; the only way you become a $20 million company is by first thinking like one, and that means changing how we think and do things."

Barb cut in. "We need cash to grow. That's the only vision I need from you. That's why he needs to go back as a technician so we can start billing his time."

"You're not seeing the big picture, mom. You and dad have done a great job with the company. In thirty years you grew it, but you've plateaued at three million dollars and the only way you get passed that is by doing something different than what you've been doing. I know how to take us to that next level. Say what you want, but I've done the research. I've met with other CEOs and all of my networking has led me to realize that we need to change. Otherwise we're not going to grow."

And while there was truth in his words it belied the other half of the coin, the darker side. In fifteen years, the company had averaged only $2.6 million. Prior to Arthur coming aboard Tony had been trying for three years to impress his ideas to no avail; he had charisma but his actions undid his magic and as a result the company had stayed the same. Now with Arthur the situation had taken a dramatic turn. Owing to his sales stratagem, the company was expected to not only surpass three million, but also reach an unprecedented $4.6M.

Tony of course wanted the credit.

"But you didn't do it," she said, "He did. And he's also improved the morale at the company. I've never seen so many smiles."

"Mother, people don't want to be happy. They want to grow. They want to feel like they belong to something bigger than themselves; they want to feel like they are growing as individuals- that they are improving their skills and moving forward. Anyone can be happy, but feeling like you are growing is something much more."

"And yet we are doing both," she said. "He has done both! He's helped us grow, and helped everyone feel good about coming into work. He's done that. Not you."

Tony tried another way. "Why is he even here. He should not be here. He's not dating Sallie anymore. Therefore, he's not a part of this family and therefore has no place on this leadership team. I think it's time he left."

He then turned to Arthur and tried to dismiss him from the room. "Get out. You don't belong here anymore."

But Barb snapped at him. "He stays! If anyone is leaving it would be you, but I want everyone here."

"Mom, you keep thinking business is about numbers. It's not. It's about giving back. That's what I do. You can say we've grown by looking at numbers, but I've helped increase our presence in this community and beyond; we're going to be international, but it starts by building connections first and that's what I've been doing.

"This company has to be more than just a place to come and work and earn a paycheck. It needs to come alive and feel like a living breathing organism; we can't just be bean counters. We have to be stimulators. We have to inspire and become leaders in change."

"Who says so? I don't want that. I don't think you're father does. We've been running our business for thirty years and grown it because we watched the numbers; that's what we care about, not about how others view us."

He shook his head. He had tried for five years to explain it, but to no avail. She just didn't get it. She had Stockholm syndrome to the old ways; the new trend wasn't about conservatism or industrialism. It was about living an organic lifestyle, nurturing relationships, and cultivating a new healthier image; like water, younger generations were about fluidity, feeling human in all activities, not just after work; companies could no longer afford to be arid. They had to be like a garden, maturing each and every plant with a rich soil of chi, engaging in spiritual yoga to harvest the bounty of nature.

Barb called it bullshit. "You will never be CEO."

He just smirked back.

Chapter 81

Struggle for Domination

Barb accused him of degeneration. "It's been five years. Five years, and you have nothing to show for it. I'm sick and tired of your bullshit. I'm tired of you wasting the company's money and time on stupid things like hosting a charity event. We're not a charity. We're a business. That's who we are. If you want to run a charity then go out and do it, but while you're at this company you sell. That's how we've grown in the past and that's how we will continue to grow. That's how every company grows, no matter how big they get. They still have to sell!"

Tony just shook his head, almost ashamed of being her son. She was such an embarrassment. "Mother, if you believe we are just about selling then why have we been on credit hold so many times with our suppliers. If you haven't changed your ways then why would you be on credit hold? It doesn't make sense. I bring in dollars, but I also do more. I work to ensure this company's future. You want me to report where I go everyday, but the reality is that I'll stop by an existing client if I'm in the area, or decide to make a cold call. It happens, and I can't call the office every second; a salesman is always on the fly, but I do far more than just sell. The question is, mother, what else do you do?

"I have enrolled you in classes, but you refused to go. Why? I'm only trying to help bring you up to speed on new advances in accounting. Why cling to the old ways when there are faster, easier, and more efficient ways to do things; you and dad both have outdated computers in the closet. Why? Get rid of those. You keep them around because you think you're going to need them. They're over twenty years old! They probably run on DOS. Get rid of them and fill that space with new technology.

"I change who I am. I educate myself. I go out and network, but what do you do? You go home after work, eat dinner, watch some television and then go to bed. That's not what somebody does who wants to grow their business; I'm out every night networking. By the time you're fast asleep I'm still out there shaking hands."

Whatever logic resided in his argument was lost by his arrogance. He flaunted his role, his successes, and the fact that he minimized her role did nothing to win her over; she critiqued his expenditures, negligence, and profit losses. He replied by pointing the finger at her as well as others, blaming everyone from the senior estimator to her.

"You can't say I haven't sold, because I have. The fact that others lose my profit is not my fault."

And therein lay the question. The company was still inexplicably strapped. There were bills unpaid, but why? How was that possible? According to the projections the company was doing outstanding. So, if there was money then why were bills not getting paid? For certain it wasn't because accounting was lazy; many suppliers offered a discount for bills paid earlier than the deadline, and 15% off was a nice incentive. So then why couldn't the bills be paid?

Barb wanted to blame Tony, but she didn't have any evidence. So something was amiss. According to the sales spreadsheets there was plenty of money coming in, and yet there wasn't any. Why? That was the question, and it's what dominated the rest of the meeting, tabling Joe yet once again.

Chapter 82

Sallie Tries to Counter

Tony resented being blamed. Despite his mother having no proof she still accused him. In the course of the meeting the two became belligerent until Sallie tried to intervene. She tried to mediate, but Tony wouldn't have it.

He accused her of conspiring against him. When she tried to resist he slammed his hand on the table and issued a list of demands; he was sick and tired of being accused of something that was clearly not his fault, and to make amends his mother and sister would apologize by fulfilling his list. First, they would provide him with a one-page report of daily figures every morning just as they did before, but had recently stopped. Next, he wanted a weekly flash report that gave him a snapshot of the week. Third, he wanted his mother's recognition of his control of HR. And lastly, he wanted Joe tabled indefinitely.

He was so loud and obnoxiously belligerent that he made Sallie cry; for a brief moment, she looked at Arthur with pitiful eyes. He had had his suspicions about why she did it, but looking into her eyes he could see it. She had never stopped loving him. Then she ran out.

Tony then turned his rage to Arthur. "I'm only going to say this once. GET THE FUCK OUT! This meeting is for owners and future owners only, and you don't belong here, so get out!"

He stared him straight in the eyes, refusing to budge. He had no intention of leaving.

"I SAID TO GET OUT. LOOK AT WHAT YOU'VE DONE TO MY FAMILY. THIS IS ALL BECAUSE OF YOU." He pointed his finger right at him, and charged him with breaking every one of the core values. "YOU'RE A DISEASE, AND I AM THE CURE."

Arthur stood up. He had had enough of this.

Chapter 83

Victor Comes Down Hard

He wasn't going to fight Tony. He was just going to leave. But as he started to Tom abruptly asked him to stay. If the coach wanted him in the room then he would stay; after all, Barb paid him and she wanted him to stay.

Meanwhile, Victor, who all this time had been on his phone, had no idea why his daughter was crying, why Tony was so angry and why his wife had her arms crossed and refused to speak with him; and this was why he avoided drama. Unbelievably, he tried to leave instead of trying to take an active role of being not just the father, but also one of the owners.

"Can you sit down," Barb asked him, more or less telling him to do it.

He looked puzzled. "I don't know what's going on. She's crying. You're grouchy. I don't know what's happening."

"That's because you're on your phone. You ignore everyone unless you want to pay attention."

Even Tony- in a rare moment- agreed with his mother. "We need you off the phone dad, because we need to figure out why we're on credit hold or for that matter why bills aren't being paid."

He looked surprised. "Why are we on credit hold? Why are bills not getting paid?" It was as though he was just joining the conversation for the very first time. Months and months of discussion, argument, and only now was Victor suddenly paying attention. It was unbelievable.

"We don't know why, Victor," said Tom, bringing him up to speed. "That's what we're trying to find out. The sales numbers are up as is service. And while there have been some issues with the project management team the profits there are largely compensatory for any losses. So, we don't really know why. Maybe you have an idea of why?"

"Look, let's just bring in more sales. That always solved the issue before."

"But sales are actually pretty good," Tom replied, rejecting that idea. "So, I actually don't think it is about sales. And if it isn't about service or operations then it must be an accounting issue, but- and I mean this will all fairness, Barb- we need to look at everything. This is a serious matter."

"Then I'll just some more techs to finish the work faster," Victor suggested, resorting to what worked in the past. "We'll get some seasonal help, or some helpers around the warehouse to speed up things. That's always done it."

But Tom wasn't so sure. "You're still having to spend money in order to make up for the money that's not there. So, I don't see how that may actually be beneficial. I like the idea, Victor, I do, and I see where you're going with it, but somewhere in our line is fumbled. It might be sales or accounting, or something else. We're not sure."

Suddenly, the topic of Joe resurfaced. Once again, it was a heated subject, but this time it warranted discussing as Joe didn't cost the company any more and by moving him back into the role of a technician the company stood to gain revenue. It was ideal. The only one rejecting it was Tony, but the others were overruling him quickly.

"Tony," the coach said, "You have to think about it this way. The company is already paying him, and until we get to the bottom of this mystery we need solutions that can help the company. What we need right now is cash. So, hear me out. Why don't we compromise? Until we figure this out Joe will *temporarily* be moved back as a technician. This will give us some billable hours to the pay the bills, and if and when we unearth this mystery then we can move him back. How does that sound?"

Chapter 84

Signatures

Tony reluctantly agreed, but lost his chances of moving Joe back after the mystery was unearthed. Moreover, Joe was eternally grateful to Arthur, who had resurfaced him at the meeting, and thus secured Joe's job. Up until that point Joe was certain he was going to be fired.

* * * * * * * * *

A few days later the mystery was unearthed, and Tony lost all chances of returning Joe back into sales. It wasn't embezzlement like some suspected. It was worse: Tony had been counting contracts that were *still* pending signatures; embezzling required there to be money first, but in this case Tony was calculating money that didn't yet belong to the company. In one example, he claimed nearly

$311,000 in quarterly bookings. Of that, only $172,000 was signed contract dollars; in the quarter before that he claimed almost $293,000, but only $67,000 of it was real.

No wonder the bills couldn't be paid! Of that last figure of $293,000 a whopping $226,000 didn't even exist; and amazingly, Tony was claiming to be the company's top salesman. It was unbelievable. Arthur discovered it and right away Barb had her proof. All at once, she rained fire and brimstone down upon her son.

"HOW DO YOU EXPECT ME TO PAY THE BILLS WHEN I DON'T HAVE THE MONEY. I NEED PROPER NUMBERS!!!!"

To her incredible surprise, he said, "Pending numbers *are* just as good as signed contracts."

Chapter 85

"A" Players

When the company suddenly knew why it couldn't pay the bills it turned on Tony, but the self-proclaimed visionary shot right back; he refused to take any blame; besides, he had a movement behind him. How would that look to the community if she actually fired him?

"A visionary can't be limited," he said, insisting that pending contracts were just as creditable as signed one; how he thought ghost figures were acceptable into accrue accounting was a mystery.

"WHAT WORLD ARE YOU LIVING ON," Barb replied, fuming; she was beyond exasperated. "Accrue accounting is projecting ahead with *anticipated* money, not with pending contracts. Those aren't the same thing! How do you not know this? You've been working here for nearly 6 years! How could you possibility think they are the same thing? How? HOW DO YOU NOT KNOW THIS? TELL ME HOW YOU DON'T KNOW THIS!"

But he just shook his head, always the arrogant son, always with all the answers. "I have to disagree. Both are operating on the assumption that money will be there, and my contracts always come through."

"But the client hasn't signed it yet, which means they can always pull out. You should know this already! You can't report what you don't already have; you can't do that. You just can't do that. When you report it we think we have the money and so we go to pay the bills but there's no money; there's no deposits. There's nothing! I need a signature. That's what I need!"

"No you don't," he replied. "You just need to be better at budgeting, which is why I enrolled you into those courses that you refused to attend. This is not my fault. It's yours for not being willing to grow and learn."

"You arrogant son-of-a-bitch! I don't have to leave anything to you! I don't have to give you this company or even leave it to Sallie, because you've got your finger wrapped around her so tightly that you'd just force her into giving it to you; well it won't happen! From now on don't you dare report a single thing until I see that signature on that contract."

"Mom, you're just not listening. A pending contract from me is like a signature already; I'm good for it. My clients always sign with me, but I completely agree with you that from anyone else, like Arthur, a signature is absolutely needed. His sales can't be trusted. I'm constantly on him to get a signature, but from me you can always count on the fact that the client will sign."

"So, where's the money," Sallie said, suddenly jumping into the argument; if anyone else was as livid it was she. If he claimed his clients always signed then where was the money? "I just looked through the system and there's no money for contracts that are four months old. Four months! We've had these contracts for an entire quarter thinking we had the money and there's no money; how do you expect us to pay the bills? It has nothing to do with budgeting you piece of shit, because there's no money!"

His eyes rolled. "My contracts always sign."

"But four months, Tony. Four!"

"What comes first, the chicken or the egg, Sallie? Answer me that. You have to budget our expenses better. If you don't have the money yet then you can't spend it. It's common sense; this is why I signed you up for those classes. I need you to be better than this. I need you to not be so stupid. Don't hold this company back like mom and dad. You need to realize that just because you see figures on a report doesn't mean you go out and spend all the money. You need to be more fiscally sound."

"You're such an asshole. You won't admit you've screwed up, so you try and turn it on us. Well fuck you. This is your fault! You did this to us. You gave us contracts that are completely worthless. We have to pay the bills and yes, I'm going to spend the money because according to the report it looks like there is money. Why would I ever assume the money isn't really there? If you're so great at being a sales manager then why don't you know that; why don't you take yourself to some of those classes and learn how to report better!"

But Tony wouldn't cave. He stood by his decision no matter how infuriated others got. For an hour he defended his actions, lauded his brilliance, and glorified his role as the company's visionary; he reiterated his charity and how it had mobilized the community. He took credit for every success of the company, including its early years, praising his pre-natal existence as his parent's muse.

He patronized their anger by accusing them of unwarranted belligerence; the charges against him were nothing more than whines from a tenderfoot. He belittled them; minimizing their efforts with such condescending

319

tone that Sallie stormed out of the office and his mother locked herself in her office. He knew he was right; he understood business better than anyone. If only they would listen to him. If only they would just listen.

And as they left he turned on Arthur. "I'm making an executive decision. Effective immediately, you are hereby terminated." But Arthur didn't budge. Instead, he simply got up, walked calmly to Barb's office, knocked on the door, and was let in. Inside, he asked her if she wished to dismiss him. When she said no he went back to his desk and continued working.

Tony tried to force him to go, even pulling the keyboard away from him. But Arthur didn't reply. He just kept his cool and allowed Tony to take whatever he wanted except whatever was on him. And that included the keys.

When he refused to give up his keys to the office Tony dialed Tom and put him on speaker. Since he had refused to surrender his keys, Tony charged him with violating the core values of being a Team Player and Promoting Growth by not quitting already. Tom failed to see the connection. So he accused him of other things.

"He has been reaching out to business owners and asking to see their operation."

"How is that a bad thing? I can't imagine how it is. Seeing what someone else is doing right can only be a good thing."

"Except that he's talking with these owners. That's not his business to do that. That's mine. As the sales manager I distribute all leads, which includes contacting anyone outside this company. He should not be talking to anyone except who I tell him to."

"Tony, I'm not following you. Networking is a part of business and as I understand it your dad, Arthur, you, and even Joe were networking. So you have four people at the company meeting others and getting leads. How is this a bad thing?"

"It's a matter of trust, Tom."

"Explain."

"What we have here is a clear violation of trust, because he has ignored the chain of command by not giving me his contacts. As the sales manager I am responsible for all figures in and out of this company and that includes all leads, which also means any contacts. By him not giving me his network contacts he has violated our core values of being a team player, promoting growth, being proactive as well as failing to demonstrate an exemplary work ethic."

According to Tony, any and all communication outside of the company was his exclusive right. While he still welcomed employees networking he insisted that they turn over any contacts they made; the right to interact with other CEOs was strictly for owners and future owners. Thus, by Arthur not only holding onto his contacts made through networking but also by talking to them he had violated a number of core values. Tom was speechless.

"Okay... but again, I'm failing to see why this is a bad thing. I don't see how it is malicious."

"I certainly welcome everyone to network. I think it's something we need to be doing more; I network all the time, wherever I'm at, even at restaurants, because you never know who your waiter knows; and think about it. How many tables does he or she serve a night? They meet all sorts of people, which makes them an untapped resource. So I'm not against anyone networking. But those contacts can become sales opportunities, which means they are leads and I distribute leads."

"That makes zero sense to me," he replied. "If Arthur networks then he has the relationship. As the sales manager it's your job to ensure he pushes that relationship in order to generate leads. That's the whole point of networking."

"And I'm happy to push him, because I believe that when we drive ourselves we discover our untapped potential. But it's also important to remember that as the sales manager I'm responsible for all the money decisions."

"No, that's Barb's job. Your job is to bring in the sales and she makes the decision what to do with that money. That's how it works. She runs the finances and you help bring in the sales. Everyone has a job to do."

"If that's the case, then I just don't see why he should be arranging visits with other CEOs. That's not his job. If I'm in charge of sales I should be doing the visits and seeing how other's run their operation to improve our sales. That's what makes sense to me."

"Tony, I'm going to have to let you go here in a second because I just got to another client's place, but if Arthur is an executive, which he is, then he has every right to visit with others so long as it has the blessing of the CEO. The truth can be said with anyone at the company. A technician even, with the CEOs blessing, could also visit because who's to say they can't learn from it or see something different that might work; we all see the world from different perspectives and pooling those perspectives together can only promote the business better."

This was preposterous. Whoever heard of such lunacy? "So Tom, let me get this straight. Someone that is on the executive team right now making executive decisions can reach out to other executives of other businesses in an attempt to grow the company?"

"Absolutely. Of course they can. If Arthur visits a place and learns how to do something better than how does that not help promote the company. It's not only being proactive but also being resourceful. He's taking what others are willing to show him and giving it back to the company. I couldn't think of anything more about promoting growth or being a team player than that."

This phone call had clearly backfired. Tony had intended to publicly scorn Arthur, but instead he had been humiliated. That wasn't right. He was a visionary. It was his job to inspire others, to be the idea generator. It was Arthur's job like everyone else to listen and obey.

"I'm gonna have to let you go, Tony. We can talk about this later."

But then Tony hit on an idea. "Real quick, I think the problem is here is that these weren't his contacts. As you said, we build relationships with whom we network with, but he has arranged these visits with those that are in fact my contacts. What's he actually done here is simply piggybacked off of my contacts."

Tom could see exactly where this was headed. "Tony, the important thing is that the company is benefiting from the visits. Whoever goes really isn't that important. It's what is learned."

Chapter 86

Scheduling Visits

After failing to convince Tom, Tony tried to persuade his father. But that also backfired. Victor was quite pleased that Arthur had taken the initiative. "Stop being so paranoid, Tony. Be proud of him instead."

* * * * * * * *

Shortly afterwards, Tony had Arthur's desk area closed in with cubicles; it initially had been open. When Arthur changed it Tony flew into a rage, throwing one of his biggest temper tantrums ever; he was apparently the company's interior decorator. He ordered him to put it back like it was, but Arthur refused.

Barb came over to investigate. She took Arthur's side, agreeing with how it was; she was never one for cubicles. She had always given her employees the option of having them or not. Some preferred it. Others didn't; whatever improved production was all she cared about.

"I like it. It's more breathable now," she said.

But Tony wouldn't have it. Immediately, he pulled several technicians who were busy preparing their trucks to cube Arthur's desk. But no sooner had they obeyed then Arthur picked it up and moved it away. "Don't you fucking touch another panel," Tony screamed at him. "If I want you in a cubicle that's where you're going! If everyone in this company would just stop and listen to me and do as I say then we could start going in the right direction!"

But no matter how many times he cubed in Arthur the panels were removed; until Barb said otherwise Arthur kept it the way he wanted.

Enraged, Tony called up Arthur's scheduled visits and cancelled them. Then secretly he set up his own.

Chapter 87

Shock and Awe

Arthur's visits had been intended for others to go, just not he. He had arranged for Barb to meet with the CEOs, Sallie to meet with other accountant managers, and Victor to meet with whomever he wished; even the senior estimator and Antonio had been invited. Tony went alone.

* * * * * * * *

Not only did Tony go alone, but he also refused to share anything he learned. To add insult to injury, he dumped $2,400 worth of receipts on his mother's desk for reimbursement. How had he spent that much on visits? These were just local companies. It's not like he flew anywhere? Arthur's planned visits were only going to cost gas and maybe a quick bite for lunch.

But Tony refused to argue. He wanted to be paid back and was in no mood to debate the issue; if she couldn't find the money to pay him then Sallie could go unpaid for a week. It was that simple.

"Are you serious! You want me to take it out of your sister's pay? How did you spend this kind of money? You don't bring me signed contracts and you spend this kind of money and I still have to figure out how to pay the bills. What the hell are you trying to do with my business?"

But Tony was already out the door. There was something that needed to be done; if nobody was going to do it then he would. Once again, the fat would be cut from the lean. He called Arthur and Sallie into the conference room and proceeded to fire him as his sister as a witness.

"You will never reach out to my contacts ever again. You will only reach out to any contacts if I give you permission. Is that understood?"

Arthur had been advised on this situation. A few days earlier he had phoned a friend who strongly suggested he simply agree to whatever Tony said. Undoubtedly it would hurt his pride, but no matter what agree.

"Thank you for obeying me," he said, abruptly pleased at his unexpected compliance. "I expect this level of obedience daily. When I said bark you bark. When I say you sell you sell. You belong to me. I own you and you will do as I say. Now, this is a lead for you," he said, handing him a slip of paper. There was a name on it. "I want you to reach out to him and get his business."

Arthur recognized the name. It was one of Tony's contacts. The visionary was setting him up. "You just said I couldn't reach out to any of your contacts?"

"I'm giving you permission."

"I refuse."

"Excuse me?"

"You heard me. I'm not going to do it."

"Are you disobeying me? That's insubordination. That is also not being a team player or helping promote this company, which means I can terminate you right here and now." Classic Tony. Bait and trap. "Perhaps we need to discuss your current employment here."

"I don't care. I'm not taking it."

"I am your boss, and you will obey me!"

"I'm not going to take it."

"You will take it! I said so."

Arthur knew better. It was a landmine and he wasn't about to step on it. "Your parents hired and only they can fire me."

"I am the sales manager and you are a salesman. So yes, I am your boss and I can fire you."

"I report to your mom and dad, not to you."

"No, you work for me and you will do as I say! I pay you, which means I can tell you what to do!"

"You don't pay me. Your mother does." And he walked out the door.

Chapter 88

Tug-of-War

At the next executive meeting, Victor began by thanking Arthur. He credited him for the company's successes and gave him his word that he would always have a seat on the leadership team. Tony shifted uncomfortably.

* * * * * * * *

The visits to other CEOs continued, as did the receipts. Enthralled by other's success, Tony bought all new furniture and set up more leases, neither of which he had permission to do. Then he went a step further by creating a business plan for expansion and sending word out to the company's suppliers that this was happening. At once, it prompted concern. If the company couldn't pay its bills how was it expanding?

But nothing slowed down Tony. He put the pen in his mother's hand and ordered her to sign it. "This is an important step in helping me be able to synchronize the global economy," he said. She just looked at him like he was an idiot. Fortunately, the plan was rejected by the venders, who had to consent seeing as though they had stake in the matter. They argued the plan was not dollar specific; it was too lofty and didn't have any tangible goals. So, Tony redrafted it and once again put it in front of his mother. However, this time she refused to sign it.

"You can shove this up your ass."

"Mother, when companies grow this increases the demands on the market, which leads to more jobs. So actually, by you not signing it you are inadvertently holding back the economy of this great country. So not only is it your duty to help promote our growth, but also this country as a whole."

"Oh, don't give me that crap. What money is there to grow? I don't see any, and until I see actual money I'm not signing a damn thing."

"I think you're missing the point," he said. "We need to be better, and by growing we become better. Like the sun, I help things grow. That's all I want to do here. I just want to make things grow. I want to give this company a new direction, and if that's a crime then I'm guilty as charged. All I want to do is inspire."

"Oh, blow it out your ass."

Moreover, at a closer glance his expansion plan revealed his long-coveted agenda. In addition to completely overhauling the entire company through restructuring, including the dismissal of Antonio, he named himself as CEO with his parents subordinate to him; all financial decisions were to be centralized through him, and every department would report to him.

Moreover, the executive team was to be abolished, because as CEO he would interact with Tom exclusively. In addition, he would receive an annual salary of $750,000 with first right to any bonuses, meaning that he was rewarded first for inspiring any employee to strive hard.

Barb wanted to punch him. Had he completely lost his mind? Why on earth would she sign it? She ordered him to redraft it or let it go. And so, he drafted a third plan. But despite it being more agreeable she still refused it.

In retaliation he replaced the company's website with a brand new one, marketing himself as the company's CEO and listing all of the branch offices on it.

Chapter 89

Collateral Damage

Tony later replaced the name "branch office" to field office, but the address remained the same. He even included a picture of it on the website. It was the home of his partner and he; he made himself CEO of that office.

* * * * * * * *

Sallie did whatever it took to relieve stress. She did yoga. She emptied a bottle of wine with her mother, and even vented to Arthur, often by sleeping with him. Nearly every day she confided in him her feelings for him; she neither begged his forgiveness nor asked him to come back to her, but Arthur understood. She couldn't risk having her heart torn apart again; she still loved him. It was her brother she feared.

Arthur suspected that somehow Tony had had a hand in the breakup, and Sallie didn't feel strong enough to tell her brother off; he always won. There was never a fight Tony ever lost. He always got his way. And so, she kept her nightly visits a secret, tucking herself into him and feeling his warmth; with him she felt reassured. She laid her head on his chest and felt the world was right. Her only regret was that the sun would rise.

"I don't hate him because he's gay," she said. "I hate him because of how he treats others. He pretends to care, but he really doesn't. He just wants control." She looked into his eyes; her troubles sank. "You are so good to me. Why? I've been so terrible to you."

He shrugged. It was just who he was.

"You've done so much for our family. I only wish my father did something." But that was wishful thinking, and she knew it. Victor stayed far away from drama; he had shouting matches with Tony, but always capitulated later.

She sighed and laid her head back down. "I wish he would put his foot down. I just wish he would tell Tony to shut up, but who am I kidding, he won't." She felt despondent, alone in the world; as long as she had Arthur she had something though. She kissed him. "I just want my brother back. Is that so much to ask for? I hate him. I wish I didn't, but I do. Why can't he see what he does to others? Why is he like this? He's like the devil reincarnate." A tear started to roll down her cheek. "I can't do this anymore. I'm physically and mentally drained."

Chapter 90

Creditors and Debtors

In recognition for his efforts, Barb and Tom thanked Arthur with a small plaque. "You have earned my deepest thanks," she said, encouraging him to display it proudly on his desk. The engraving on it acknowledged him as the builder of the company's vision, growth, and culture. When Tony saw it however he demanded it be taken down at once; he took one look at it curiously and stormed away. When Arthur refused he again threatened to fire him.

"If your parents wish me to go then I will."

But Tony just shook his head. "That's not how it works here. You are a salesperson and I am your sales manager, and you will obey me! And if you don't meet my quota that I set for you then you're outta here." He then set the number at the ridiculous amount of $720,000, which perhaps at the start of the year might have been feasible, but not halfway in. But Arthur remained confident; he would do the impossible, if that's what it took, and later that day one of his clients called to award him the largest contract the company had ever received, $5 million.

<u>Chapter 91</u>

Growing Pains

While Arthur humbly took pride in the largest contract the company had ever had, Tony paraded through the office gloating his nearly $240,000 in pending contracts.

* * * * * * * *

Arthur owed much to Victor and Barb. He had grown as a person and as a professional. With the former, he had become a salesman that clients now asked for and felt confident with him at the helm; in just a short time his reputation was at its highest. He had major clients calling him up and asking for him; they refused to do business with Tony, even going so far as to say they only wished to do business with someone they had heard of.

With Barb's trust, Arthur had been given a rare opportunity to oversee an entire company's growth. She had vested in him incredible power and privilege, and in return he realized her dream. From a stagnating $2.6 million to a fledging $9.6 million, he had achieved what she had always wished for. "You gave me the greatest dream ever," she said, shedding a tear knowing the only better dream would be having him as her son-in-law. "You listened, you learned, and you showed respect. I couldn't ask for anything more. Thank you. From the bottom of my heart, thank you."

But she knew it was only a matter of time. Tony always got his way, and somehow, in some horrible way, he would twist her arm and oblige her to fire him.

Chapter 92

Perspectives

Tony tried numerous times to fire him, often citing new violations against the core values. He accused him of sabotaging his sales, of hogging all the leads, and of industrial espionage. "You're hogging all the leads that come into the office," he said, "and that means your hurting my numbers as well as everyone else's! We could all have booked more business if you weren't trying to steal them for yourself."

"But you distribute them."

"That's right, but you're answering the phone. So from now on you don't answer the phone unless I say so."

"And if someone calls me on my cell?"

"You can answer that, but you don't get to pursue any leads until I say you can. From now on, anyone who calls you must go through me first. Is that understood?"

Arthur agreed; he was still following the advice given to him, but his compliance only made matters worse. Tony stopped filtering leads. Arthur's entire sales strategy and the reason for why the company had succeeded so well depended entirely upon filtered leads. Tony however felt it wasn't his job to filter leads, so he passed them off; all of a sudden he was now taking every lead that came in and dumping them onto Arthur.

"I expect you to follow up on every last one."

It was clear what he was doing. The whole point of filtering was that whoever received the lead via phone or email then filtered it according to how Arthur had trained everyone. Ask questions and get specific information. If the potential client wasn't willing to divulge that or was simply shopping around then the lead was dropped. Once filtered, the lead could be passed on; it all came down to time and money.

But Tony didn't see it that way. He felt his time was more important than the team's. And so in addition to distributing unfiltered leads he also issued them late. Thus, even if a lead had been good it was now too late to close the deal. Nevertheless, Tony still took credit for them. But when Arthur miraculously salvaged a $440,000 deal Tony abruptly required his review of it as the sales manager. He then kept it on his desk for nearly six weeks without ever looking at it. Not surprising, the client went elsewhere.

He then continued to accuse Arthur of violating the core values, including hacking into his email. "That is a complete violation of honesty and goes against the policies of this company!" The fact that he had given him his email login and password was completely ignored. Nevertheless, the severity of it warranted an investigation. And so, Barb called an immediate meeting with Arthur and Victor.

Tony demanded to be present, but she refused.

"Tell us your side," she said, believing him to be innocent of the charges. While he talked Victor ate out of a can of mixed nuts, paying as little attention as possible. He shared with them Tony's recent list of demands, including distributing unfiltered leads and requiring permission to do anything. He added that as sales manager Tony had said that he had every right to tell him what to do or he could be fired; to Barb's horror, Arthur shared what Tony had said to him and how he had been trying to fire him on several occasions.

"He said that since he pays me that I have to obey him; that because he is the sales manager he can tell me what to do."

Victor looked up. "Who said that? Not my son."

"Where have you been?" Barb said, irate at him. "Put those away and pay attention. This is what I've been dealing with and I need you to listen!"

Victor looked confused. He thought this meeting was to fire Arthur. He went for more nuts.

"I said put those down!" She took it from him.

"Hey, I was eating that."

"Haven't you been listening to a word he's been saying?" His obliviousness was intolerable.

"Aren't we firing him? Why do we need to have a meeting to do that? Just show him the door."

She slammed her fist down on the table. "We're not firing him! If there were anyone I would fire it would be Tony. Now pull your head out of your ass and start paying attention!"

Surprise wiped across his face. Why would she fire their son? That made no sense. Hadn't Tony grown the company like he said? What had Arthur done? If Sallie didn't want him it was probably because he was a bum.

"Why would you fire Tony? He's grown this company and proven he can take over when I retire."

"Are you senile? Tony didn't do anything. It has all been Arthur. This young man has done everything, not Tony. He's done it all." And with that she brought him up to speed; as she laid fact after fact at his feet the mountain of atrocities grew and Victor's jaw dropped; in twenty minutes he got nearly six years of disaster, negligence, incompetence, and irresponsibility. She even explained how Tony had been networking himself as the CEO and that's why the master of ceremony had said that; his charity event was nothing short of self-promotion.

Victor's was aghast. He hesitated to believe any of it, but it was coming from Barb, and there was nobody he trusted more than her; despite his affair, she had always remained true to him, never lying, always being honest. He had no reason to distrust her.

"You need to put your foot down and get him straightened out," she said, detailing his purges, his expenditures, his repeated abuses of the core values and how he had even forced her to empty the company's cash just to host his charity event. "Your idiot son is bankrupting us! Why do you think I don't have any money to pay the bills, because he either takes it all or spends it, and none of his contracts actually have signatures on them; I have no money! Do you understand? I have no money.

"We're on credit hold, because that idiot son of ours thinks he can do whatever he wants and thinks that contracts without a signature are just as good as contracts with signatures. Do you realize I haven't collected rent for nearly six years simply because of how stupid his decisions have been? He's ruining us!"

"That's an exaggeration."

"Is it?"

She added that Tony altered the performance reviews just to publicly shame her, and if that wasn't evidence enough she told him that he was no longer doing his own quotes. From what Antonio had confided in her Tony was having the estimating and service departments do his quotes. No wonder why everyone is falling behind!"

"But he's supposed to be doing his own?"

"Tell that to him!"

She opened a spreadsheet to prove her point. It showed the figures of the sales team. Not surprisingly, both Antonio and the senior estimator had the lowest count.

"Do you see? And he accuses them of underperforming. That's why he keeps pushing us to fire your brother and him. He overworks them to death. He's a slave driver. How could they possibly expect to do their jobs when they're doing Tony's, and what is our idiot son doing instead. He's out, running around doing his charity thing.

"Are you getting this now," she asked, venting it all out. "Are you seeing what's been happening? But if it weren't for Arthur we would have already gone bankrupt. It was him that saved us. He's done it all."

"So why are we having a meeting with him and not Tony? This is a waste of time!"

"Have you listened to a word I've said? Tony is trying to fire the one person who is keeping you and me and everyone else employed here. It has been his sales approach that gave us these numbers; he's never asked for anything in return, but what has he gotten instead? Sallie broke up with him, and I'll bet Tony had something to do with that. And now he's been accused of hacking. For something that has given his heart to this place all he's ever gotten in return is a kick in the ass."

It was too much for Victor. But Barb was on a roll. She was only getting started. She pointed to Tony's numbers on the spreadsheet. "Look at all these. They're all pending signatures, every last one of them."

"Then why are they being counted?"

"Exactly. Why? That's what I want to know too."

"But what about his numbers," he said, asking to see Arthur's numbers. Clearly, there had to be something of fault. After all, Arthur wasn't perfect. But whereas Tony had "earned" the company dollars, Arthur's contracts had signatures. Of Tony's $293,000 there was still $226,000 of it still pending. On the other hand, Arthur's nearly $242,000 were all signed and at a profit margin of 57%, which amounted to almost $138,000.

"And what he estimates he gets, or does better. That's how good Arthur is," she told him. "So if he says he's going to earn the company this then I believe him."

It was clear that the wheels were turning, though slowly. He asked her to scroll down. The senior estimator's numbers were a paltry $165,000.

"Wait, why is that so low? It should be higher."

Hadn't he been listening? "You're right. It should, but again that's because Tony is asking him to write his quotes for him instead of doing them himself."

Victor leaned back, stupefied. He had entered this meeting on an apparently wrong assumption, and now he was too overwhelmed to catch up; all this time he had believed Arthur had been the problem. Now he was too disorientated to think; it was all crashing down on him. So it wasn't Arthur that was the problem, but Tony. He tried to wrap his head around it, but it was too big.

It was never Arthur. It was their son. Like a great awakening, Victor was speechless, lost for words. Despite all the evidence in front of him he still wished to deny it; it was more than he could comprehend. So, Tony was the problem, not Arthur. All of the company's financial problems were a direct result of Tony. He struggled to believe it, but Barb had all the numbers to prove it.

He stood up. Not saying a word he walked out. He had meant to retire, but now that seemed impossible. Of all the problems he had ever solved as an owner this was one he felt he couldn't. He felt vexed. He wanted to look the other way, but somehow he couldn't now. But if Tony was indeed the problem could it be fixed? Could Tony be changed? And if not, could he do what was necessary? Could he fire his son?

Chapter 93

Sales Philosophy

Victor drank himself to sleep that night. Of all the problems in the world this was not one he wanted. All he wanted to do was retire. Frustration turned to anger and he bitterly resented his wife as well as Arthur for dumping this on him. Sometimes ignorance is bliss.

* * * * * * * *

Barb was eternally grateful for Arthur. He had helped to open Victor's eyes, but whether he would do anything or not was a good of a guess as any. Sadly, she felt he would do nothing. And when Tony learned that Arthur was still employed he publicly disparaged her. He shamed her and accused her of violating the core values: by not firing Arthur she was not promoting growth.

351

She rarely slept now. Every night she emptied a bottle of wine and in the morning drank three to four cups of coffee; she came to work as little as possible, attending yoga classes instead. She tried to meditate, but Tony's voice kept shouting at her; the weaker she became the more he took advantage of that.

He had a heavyset female employee switch desks with a petite one, just because he thought the woman's weight might scare away customers. "We need to present ourselves as a healthy company," he said. He then moved the heavier woman further back into the office. "I noticed the ground wasn't level near my car in the parking lot. So I think we need to balance the foundation by putting you closer in the middle."

He then proceeded to fire everyone in accounting, blaming Sallie for crying all of the time. "We can't have such negligence if we expect to grow."

"Fuck you, you asshole. You try paying bills when your idiot brother doesn't get signatures."

"That's not being a team player, Sallie. I would really hate to have to fire you."

"I'll quit before you do. You're so fucking stupid. All you think of is yourself. You don't realize how dumb all of your decisions are, and if you want to fire me for trying to do my job then I'll fire you for being such a dumbass."

His smirk did nothing to disarm her. And neither did his next demand. He insisted that accounting accept his mysterious formula for holding sales agents accountable to seven times what they cost the company. Why the number seven, nobody knew. But Barb had her suspicions. Tony was all about revenue, not profit. If Arthur had to book $750,000 a year just to pay for himself- according to Tony- then this was easier to do with revenue. And Tony wished to continue to count his pending signatures.

Chapter 94

A High Price Tag

As predicted, Tony counted his pending contracts towards his seven-number formula. Instantly, giving himself the title of top salesman. "As you can see, I am not only the company's sales manager, but also it's visionary and future."

* * * * * * * *

In addition to hiring Tom, Barb was also obliged to hire a new outside accounting firm. But whereas Tom cost the company $54,000 a year this firm broke the bank. Each of its partners charged her $415 an hour, even if one of the firm's junior associates were helping her; they claimed a "supervision fee." Moreover, the firm sent along two associates during the first two weeks to familiarize themselves with the company's finances. The bill was high.

At $250 an hour per associate as well as the supervisory fee the invoice came to an astonishing $26,000 for those two weeks. That averaged to $325 an hour in an eight-hour day, in just two weeks! Thus, within just the first month alone Barb had spent nearly half as much as she was spending on Tom… and she had Tony to thank for that.

Chapter 95

Vacancies

"Visionaries build the world," Tony said, taking credit for the company's success right before announcing he was taking a well-earned vacation. He went abroad and visited a manufacturer that the company did not do business with. Nevertheless, he asserted it was a business trip and insisted on being reimbursed. Of his twelve days abroad only 2 hours had been spent at the factory. The trip had cost him $11,000.

* * * * * * * *

Tom tried to remind Barb and Victor that they were the owners, but that was easier said than done. With Tony, it was either his way or the highway. Although he wasn't the owner, he certainly ran it like he was.

The more she clashed with Tony the weaker she got and consequently the less energy she had to protest. Then one day, it finally happened. She broke. Arthur was out on a sales call when he got a call from her. She told him he was no longer on the executive team. In the background he could hear Tony's voice telling her what to say.

Chapter 96

Renewing Contracts

Victor now stopped attending the leadership meetings. He was neither interested in them nor cared about remedying his son's behavior. He also did nothing to restore Arthur to the team.

* * * * * * * *

Tom phoned Barb to inform her that he would not be renewing his contract. She begged him to reconsider, but he declined. The writing was on the wall, and there was no turning back now. Besides, he preferred clients that were stable and the company was verging on bankruptcy it sounded like. How could she possibly keep it afloat?

He also stated that Tony was another reason. He had dealt with plenty of Tony-like characters in the past, but companies were often large enough to sustain such eccentric personalities; Barb's company was not. To make matters worse, Victor was no longer participating and this was problematic because while she was the CEO the two of them were still the owners. And if Arthur was no longer on the team than this left only Sallie and her.

"I don't think we might have very productive meetings. So, that's another reason why."

"Please, I need you to stay. We can work something out, but I feel you've been a big part of this."

He sighed over the phone. It wasn't hard to hear her plea. He wasn't one to get emotionally involved, but he certainly understood her pain. Perhaps it was all those in the past that he had abandoned that made him reconsider; he paused to think it over. The writing was on the wall. That was clear as day. But until it closed he decided to be a bit greedy. If she wanted him that badly it would cost her.

Chapter 97

Blank Checks

Barb was overjoyed as she put the phone down. Tom said he would think it over, and that if he agreed he strongly suggested they limit the meetings to exclusively her and him. Tony was out as well as Sallie. She agreed.

As she waited for his decision she dealt with Tony trying to fire his sister. He tried to exclude her from the succession plan. "What I need is a compliant operations manager, not a business partner." But when that failed he tried to dismiss her from the executive team. When that also failed he tried to fire Frank and replace him with Troy as the new superintendent. When that too failed he stormed into his mother's office and demanded five blank checks a week. "I have to work without constraint of limitation."

"Not on my dime mister. You can forget it."

"Mother, please," he said, shaming her. "The fact is that supervisors deserve credit first before anyone else. I run many departments here, and if anyone should get a plaque it's me. I've done more for building this company's culture, its vision and its future than anyone."

Chapter 98

Capitulation

After her brother tried to fire her Sallie went to her dad, but Victor did nothing. He refused to intervene. "You can always work elsewhere if you don't like it here."

* * * * * * * *

With morale once again eroding and the company verging on bankruptcy, Tony decided that the best solution was by ordering his sister and mother to reallocate monies away from the technicians and the fleet and instead put it towards financing his charity, which had become a fledging movement by now.

"We are building the drive for our future."

Instead of selling he now spent more of his time chairing committees to expand the charity's efforts; he was the chair, but he was never around for any meetings. He also networked, but not on behalf of the company but rather to gain sponsorships and connect local businesses. He joined other CEOs for breakfast, lunch and dinner, submitting his receipts for reimbursement, and earning the company nothing.

He laughed heartedly and enjoyed himself, eating sushi and drinking wine. "When we open our hearts," he said spiritedly, "we inspire not only the good in ourselves, but also the good in our community and the businesses and trades that make it up. We are truly a global community."

He neglected his departments and instead spent time on the golf course, smoking cigars and shaking hands; he refused to give technicians water but insisted they worked hard so that he could enjoy his happiness. "You work so that I can pursue my happiness, because that's the American dream."

<u>Chapter 99</u>

Pleading

Tom agreed to renew his contract with Barb, but at an additional cost of $18,000, which now equated to $1,000 an hour.

* * * * * * * *

Six months after breaking up with him, Sallie finally confessed. She surprised Arthur at his apartment. As soon as he opened the door she fell to her knees and threw her hands into the prayer position. Tears streamed down her face; she could bear it no longer. She begged him to take her back.

"I'm so sorry," she said, confessing what he had suspected all along. "He made me do it. I can't argue with him anymore. I have no choice but to do whatever he asks.

He is my older brother and his happiness is more important than mine. Please, please, forgive me."

She pleaded with him to not only take him back but also to listen and obey Tony. "It's the only way. If he's happy then so can we, but his happiness is the only way."

"You have a choice," he replied. "His happiness doesn't have to come before yours. You deserve to be happy, and I want you to be happy, but I won't give up my happiness for someone else. I can't do that."

"Not even for me."

"How can I be happy when I have to give up part of my soul? I was happy with you, but I can't be if you put your happiness second to Tony's. I love you for you are, not for half of you." He had wanted to marry her. He wanted a family, but how could he have that if she was always putting her brother's happiness first. Everyone deserved the right to pursue happiness. It wasn't exclusive to Tony alone. But it was even more than that. He could see it in her eyes. She just needed an ally, not a friend, partner, or lover. If she still loved him she would never have asked him that; he knew her better than that. Sadly, he closed the door on her.

A. Ruben

The Legal Fight

Chapter 100

Numbers

How could he take her back? The Sallie he once knew was gone. Instead of a strong, independent woman with goals and passion she was now reduced to a hollow shell submissive to her brother's will; she continued to lose weight, almost to the point of anorexic.

* * * * * * * *

A month after he turned her away he was fired. Both Victor and Barb had the displeasure of terminating him, regretting every second of it. Barb admitted how Tony had spent the entire weekend pulling her arm as well as Victor's. There was nothing she could do. As they pulled him into the office to tell him he was fired Tony walked by with a smug on his face.

Neither was happy to see him go. He had done so much to the company. Of his $1.2 million bookings for the year as well as his $5 million deal he had earned nearly two million dollars in profit; Victor shook his hand. Arthur had been his greatest salesman ever.

Barb shed a tear. Letting him go was the hardest thing she had ever done in her career. With his help, the company had grown seven million dollars in less than two years during an economic recession, and she didn't know how to thank him; it wasn't his fault Tony was bankrupting the company. Arthur had done something impressive.

And now that he knew the truth Victor had difficulty finding the words. Arthur had been an astute pupil, learning like a sponge, impressing him at every turn. Always eager to learn, the young man had accompanied him early on to meet clients, learn the business, and through trial and error had succeeded. He made mistakes, but he learned from them; he sold, he networked, he accepted challenges and always rose to the occasion; he had been a hard worker, taking charge and being proactive instead of reactive, and always practiced what he preached.

He held himself to high expectations, imbuing a strong sense of standard into others and inspiring them into action not through words but accountability; he gave the company back its pride, restored Sallie's self-esteem if only for a short while, and gave her a level of pride that she never had before. Whereas Tony boasted about how great of a leader he was Arthur demonstrated it; as they sat across from him reading aloud the charges against him they felt their hearts break; they knew the charges to be false, but Tony had twisted their arms, refusing to let up until they capitulated.

Among the charges included hacking and stealing confidential files privy only to the executive team, which was undoubtedly against company policy if not for the fact that it was false as well as the fact that Barb had never revoked his access; in her heart, she had never expelled him and as she read the charges she cried. It was the saddest day of her life. The golden age of the company was passing.

Chapter 101

Barb's Revenge

Shortly before Arthur was dismissed, Antonio took him out to lunch a few days earlier. There he confided in him how much he feared Tony's inevitable succession. "I don't know him anymore," he said. "He's not the kid I once knew. Now he's just crazy."

* * * * * * * *

Barb resented being forced to dismiss Arthur. She hated her son for making her do it; it wasn't right. If anyone was to be fired it was undoubtedly Tony. But she had a plan. It wasn't elaborate, but it had required both time and a bit of crafty ingenuity on her part; secrecy was paramount and the thought of sweet revenge helped her sleep at night.

Suspecting the worst to come she had prepared months in advance, and the final stroke of her plan came on the day they dismissed Arthur. While Tony gave a smug and began to clean out Arthur's desk, overjoyed at the prospect of finally firing him, Barb put her last step into motion. In the office, she closed the door and not only offered Arthur favorable terms of a severance but also wrote them on company letterhead, dated it, and had everyone sign it. He was then told to pocket the piece of paper on his way out; he was not to let Tony see it.

As soon as Arthur was safe away she played dumb, admitting to have forgotten to have Arthur sign a release document. As predicted, Tony went ballistic; it had occurred to her one night that his predictability could be her advantage, and thus she allowed him to rebuke her; although it hurt her pride, she was playing a much bigger game here.

Complying with Tony's demand she had Victor stop by Arthur's apartment to drop off a generic release document, printed off from the Internet. Two weeks went by and still no reply; good for him, she thought. Arthur was just as smart as she had expected: why should he sign it when he already had a contract for severance? Legally, the severance contract trumped the release document since it

371

came first, was dated, signed, and on company stationary; as far as anyone was concerned the release document was completely worthless.

But Tony knew nothing of the severance contract and so he continued to badger his mother to get the release signed. He forced her to send an email telling Arthur that if it were not signed and returned that he would forfeit any possibility of severance; Tony figured offering the prospect of a severance would be convincingly enough to get the release document signed.

All at once, Arthur had written proof of reneging and hired an attorney; upon receiving a letter the company's attorney handed it over and Tony burst into laughter. "Is he retarded? He doesn't have a case."

The company's attorney agreed. Clearly, Arthur had no case. The letter only claimed discrimination. It said nothing about any severance contract... and Barb said nothing either. She kept Tony *and* her attorney in the dark about it, and if anyone thought this was foolish then they didn't understand her level of exasperation. She was willing to sacrifice everything in order to destroy Tony.

She smiled inside, quite satisfied to let this drag out. Not only was she well aware that legal battles were expensive but she delighted in the fact that their attorney was exploitive. He once invoiced the company for $1,500 just to clear Victor of a parking ticket and two points; it took all of ten minutes to stand before the judge before it was settled. Frankly, she couldn't ask for better council.

As the weeks turned into months, Tony became irritable. The legal bills were stacking up. "You have jeopardized this company for the last time, mother," he said, smoking red fumes. "Your blatant incompetence has once again threatened everything I have done here! YOU ARE DESTROYING EVERYTHING!" But she played her poker face well.

As the months passed it became crystal clear to Arthur and his attorney that the company's attorney was in the dark; he had no knowledge whatsoever of the severance contract. Realizing this extraordinary fact they played it to their maximum advantage, allowing the pompous company lawyer to dig his own grave: they let him mock them and be disrespectful. Once he even stated in his letters that he was laughing at Arthur. He even told Arthur's attorney to pass along a message. "Tell your client he's fucking insane."

After months of snooty remarks and disparaging replies Arthur's attorney finally pulled out their ace. All at once the company's lawyer caved. Instantly apologetic, he humbly begged for mercy and expressed remorse for his rudeness. Whereas he had delayed or simply ignored their communications in the past now he was extremely responsive and ready to settle. In a complete turnaround, the man no longer doubted Arthur had a case.

Terms. Signatures. A date. Letterhead. It was a contract. No questions asked, but why had nobody told him about this. And with Barb's email regarding forfeiture of severance it was indisputably a breach of contract. At once, the company agreed to all of Arthur's modest terms. He wasn't greedy. He just wanted what was owed to him: his severance, his attorney fees paid for, and a letter of commendation from the company.

When Tony learned of the news he flew into a rage. How had he not known about the severance contract? Why had nobody told him? Why on earth would his mother not tell the attorney? Was she senile? It was undeniable proof of her negligence and evidence that it was now time to pass the torch; clearly she was no longer fit to run the company. At the next executive meeting, despite it only being Tom and her, Tony attended and coerced her to yield all executive decision-making to him; she could remain CEO, but only nominally. From this point forward, Tony was in charge. Barb had no qualms about that.

Chapter 102

The Banker

"This is all on you," he said, shaming his mother. He couldn't believe his parents had signed it. "I'm not the one who fired him. So this is all on you two!" He wiped his hands clean, thinking it was over. It was, at least for her, but not for him. As she leaned back in satisfaction she picked up a bank letter giving her all the money she would ever need.

* * * * * * * *

If revenge was a dish best served cold then Barb had Arthur to thank for that. He had given her a golden opportunity to strike back at her son: while her dream was to surpass three million dollars there was something else she wanted and that was to secure her retirement. As head of accounting she frequently interacted with the bank. Over the years the bank had become habituated to her plateau reports, but when Arthur's strategy suddenly increased the company by seven million a red flag went up. As if by fate, it just so happened that the bank's regional vice president was in the area, and he decided to investigate the matter personally. Phoning her, he asked for an explanation, which she calmly and confidently replied was all due to her new sales manager, Arthur; this occurred months prior to his dismissal. She invited the vice president to not only review any of her books but also to meet Arthur if he so wished.

She gave him the address of the networking event he was attending that night. "I'm certain you won't be disappointed in speaking with him and hearing what he has to say. If you have any further questions just let me know."

That night a tall gentleman approached Arthur and introduced himself as the regional vice president of one of the world's top ten banks. Arthur had met many CEOs and executives before, but this man clearly was going out of his way to meet him. As they talked, the man could see how genuine he was. Arthur shared stories of his adventures, told jokes that made him laugh, and when they talked business it was clear his fiscal conservatism and sound stratagem supported the reports; the man felt assured that the reports would match the books after speaking with him.

"Tell me something," he said to Arthur. "What do you see in your future? Where do you see yourself in five years?"

"Well," he replied. "I hope to one day be helping the company grow even more. I'd like to help run things with him and his sister," he said pointing to Tony. The man looked over. Tony was busy acting like a host, matching people up. But there was something else. Something didn't sit right with him. Perhaps it was Tony's over-exuberance. It was excessive, like he was a host for a college party, making sure everyone was having a good time; there was nothing wrong with anyone being happy, but Tony seemed infected with it and consequently it made his enthusiasm appear insincere; concern crossed the man's face.

It seemed Tony was more interested in earning a name for connecting people than about building solid relationships; he preferred to have likes on social media, filling a perpetual void with hollow recognition than actually getting to know somebody; he'd rather have hundreds of so-called friends than one very good best friend that knew him inside and out. He was not someone who could survive alone mentally on a deserted island; he needed an audience.

A. Ruben

The man turned back to Arthur. "Not every company is left to a son or daughter," he said, "Sometimes it can go to someone else that may run things better."

Chapter 103

The Loans

A month after Arthur was fired Troy quit. Frank followed after that, announcing his retirement.

* * * * * * * *

With the regional vice president's approval the red flag was removed and the bank went ahead issuing Barb an increase in her line of credit. At once, she took out four loans that totaled over $1,100,000. Now her retirement was secure. She'd let Tony worry about paying it back as well as those attorney invoices; if he wanted to be CEO he could, but he'd have to answer for that debt. Revenge was truly a dish best served cold, especially from a mother to a son.

Chapter 104

Another Door Opens

A few months after Arthur's dismissal, Joe called him up to tell him that Troy had quit and Frank had retired. He said Tony had gone on a hiring spree, hiring more technicians and reveling in the company's success. "It's like he's swimming in a bathtub of money. He's delusional. There's like six more techs here now, but who knows how long they'll be here," he said.

Arthur asked him if a large contract had come in. One had, and Joe was amazed by it. "It's like five million dollars," he said in disbelief. "It's huge. I can't believe you got that!" But unfortunately Tony had rejected it. "He says its best for the company this way. But I heard he didn't want it because your name was on it. Seems pretty dumb if you ask me if that's the reason. We could use the money."

Arthur wanted to say something, but thanked him instead for the call. "You take care of yourself."

"You too," Joe said. "And thanks again for helping me. I can't tell you how much I appreciate what you did for me... and for all of us. You did a lot, so whatever you do next I know you'll do just as good."

And as one door closed another opened. At once, Arthur began receiving calls from CEOs and presidents that wanted him. Ultimately, he took an offer in Cleveland.

Chapter 105

Epilogue

Later, while in Cleveland, Arthur ran into an old vender who told him the company was struggling once again. Apparently the company was again on credit-hold; whatever string of luck they had was gone. "I remember about two years ago," the guy said, "they did really well. They had this amazing jump, but now look at them."

He added that Tony seemed to be in charge now, but it wasn't helping. "I'm not sure if his parents are fully retired, but when they do I don't think that company is going to last." He also shared with him how Tony was still running his charity and collecting humanitarian awards. "I guess it's more important than running a company and keeping people employed."

In addition, Tony's partner was also employed now, being prostituted by Tony to blog for other companies in exchange for sales leads. There was rumor that some technicians had been let go, but Arthur suspected that wasn't the case. He figured if Tony had any chance of salvaging the company it was through service. And in fact, Sallie was now the company's operation manager.

Her soul was buried. Her happiness all but gone, and apparently she had found some solace in a pet puppy, which Tony kept a litter box for it beside the desk of the heavyset woman that he moved to the middle; part of being a team player Arthur supposed incredulously. He suspected it was hardly a great place to work anymore.

"I guess that's how it is," the vender said, wishing him well. "One day you're on top of the world and the next you're not. Oh well. It is what it is."